CU00918775

Karl Barth on Religion

Karl Barth is one of the most influential theologians of the past century, especially within conservative branches of Christianity. Liberals, by contrast, find many of his ideas to be problematic. In this study, Keith Ward offers a detailed critique of Barth's views on religion and revelation as articulated in the *Church Dogmatics*. Against Barth's definition of religions as self-centred, wilful, and arbitrary human constructions, Ward offers a defence of world religions as a God-inspired search for and insight into spiritual truth. Questioning Barth's rejection of natural theology and metaphysics, he provides a defence of the necessity of a philosophical foundation for Christian faith. Ward also dismisses Barth's biased summaries of German liberal thought, upholding a theological liberalism that incorporates Enlightenment ideas of critical inquiry and universal human rights that also retains beliefs that are central to Christianity. Ward defends the universality of divine grace against Barth's apparent denial of it to non-Christian religions.

KEITH WARD is a Canon Professor at Christ Church College, Oxford and a fellow of the British Academy. The author of many books, most recently *Adventures in Belief*, he has taught at the University of Glasgow, Kings College London, where he was Professor of the History and Philosophy of Religion, and the University of Oxford, where he was the Regius Professor of Divinity.

KEITH WARD
University of Oxford

Karl Barth on Religion
A Critique

CAMBRIDGE
UNIVERSITY PRESS

Shaftesbury Road, Cambridge CB2 8EA, United Kingdom

One Liberty Plaza, 20th Floor, New York, NY 10006, USA

477 Williamstown Road, Port Melbourne, VIC 3207, Australia

314–321, 3rd Floor, Plot 3, Splendor Forum, Jasola District Centre, New Delhi – 110025, India

103 Penang Road, #05–06/07, Visioncrest Commercial, Singapore 238467

Cambridge University Press is part of Cambridge University Press & Assessment, a department of the University of Cambridge.

We share the University's mission to contribute to society through the pursuit of education, learning and research at the highest international levels of excellence.

www.cambridge.org
Information on this title: www.cambridge.org/9781009555432

DOI: 10.1017/9781009555456

First published 2025

A catalogue record for this publication is available from the British Library

A Cataloging-in-Publication data record for this book is available from the Library of Congress

ISBN 978-1-009-55543-2 Hardback
ISBN 978-1-009-55541-8 Paperback

Cambridge University Press & Assessment has no responsibility for the persistence or accuracy of URLs for external or third-party internet websites referred to in this publication and does not guarantee that any content on such websites is, or will remain, accurate or appropriate.

Contents

1 **Revelation as Sublimation**   *page* 1
Analysis of Barth's General Heading: 'The Revelation
    of God as the Sublimation of Religion'   1
Barth's Idea of Sublimation   3

2 **Barth's Theology of Religion**   7
Barth's Idea of Religion   7
    The Limited Scope of Barth's Idea of Religion   12
    Buddhism   17
Revelation and Buddhism   22
    Hinduism   27
    Devotion in Hinduism and Christianity   32
    East Asian Religions   36
    Religious Diversity and Salvation   38

3 **The Revolt against Liberalism**   41
Barth's Relation to German Liberal Theology   41
Immanuel Kant   46
Friedrich Schleiermacher   48
Adolf von Harnack   51
    The Search for Truth   54
True Religion   56

4 **The Nature of Revelation**   61
Barth's Idea of Revelation   61
    Change and Development in Religion   63
    Revelation and Certainty   65

The Case of Judaism 68
Incomplete Revelation 69
  Interpretations of Revelation 71
  The Misleading Use of Sublimation 74

5 Revelation against Religion 77
Analysis of Barth's First Chapter: 'The Problem
  of Religion in Theology' 77
  The Relation between Revelation and Religion 81
Universal Concepts of Religion 82
Uncertainties in Revelation 85
Revelation and Interpretation 89
  The Wesleyan Quadrilateral 93

6 The Failure of Religion 97
Analysis of Barth's Second Chapter: 'Religion
  as Faithlessness' 97
Revelation and Diversity 100
Good Works and Faith 104
Predestination and Compatibilism 107
Divine and Human Freedom 110
Three Incoherences 112
The Futility of Seeking God 113

7 The Failure of Philosophy 117
God and Philosophy 117
Natural Theology and Metaphysics 120
Knowing God 121
The Revelation of God in Christ 124
  Atheism and Mysticism – A Story (Very) Loosely
  Based on Fact 130

8 Religion and Truth 135
Analysis of Barth's Third Chapter: 'The True Religion' 135
The Universality of Grace 137
Godlessness and Faith 139

The Fall of Humanity 142
    A Short History of Christianity Revised 144
The Medieval Synthesis 146
'Modern Man' 148
Human Fulfilment and Liberal Christianity 150
Peniel 153

9 **Universal Grace** 159
Religions and Grace 159
Universalism 164
The Final Position? 171
Creation 173
    Election 176
The Existence of Evil 180
    Justification 183
    Sanctification 185

Select Bibliography 189
Index 193

1 | Revelation as Sublimation

Analysis of Barth's General Heading: 'The Revelation of God as the Sublimation of Religion'

I have taught in British and American universities for all of my working life. I have been successively, a professor of philosophy, a professor of the history of religion, and a professor of theology.[1] So it was inevitable that sooner or later I would have to read the works of Karl Barth. With that history behind me, it is perhaps not surprising that I found what he wrote about religion to be shocking, distressing, and deeply alien. I think he has been a bad influence on much modern theology, and that his views are in conflict with all that I had learned about religion and about Christianity during my long career.

Barth would not have been surprised by this, since I am just the sort of person he persistently attacked as 'faithless', 'demonic', and 'wilfully arbitrary' (these words are taken from *Church Dogmatics*, volume I, part 2, para. 17, on religion). I understand that he is writing Christian theology, not philosophy or comparative religion. But in this long section he is writing a Christian theology of religion, and the fact that he mentions Buddhism, Hinduism, and Judaism shows that he means to talk about a Christian view of many world religions. My intention is to analyse his text in detail, and show why

---

[1] I was a professor for the longest time at King's College, London University, where I was Professor of the Philosophy of Religion and Head of the Department of Religious Studies, and at Christ Church, Oxford University, where I was the Regius Professor of Divinity.

I was distressed and shocked by it. I will also show how there can be a very different Christian theology of religion, and that a more liberal Christian view, which he set out to oppose in its German forms, has much to recommend it.

In a much later work, delivered as a lecture to a meeting of Swiss Reformed ministers in 1956, he spoke of a 'change of direction in the thinking of evangelical theology'.[2] This change, he said, was not in opposition to his earlier work, which entails that in an important sense what he wrote in the early section of the *Dogmatics* remains in force. He also remarked that he had indulged in some 'exaggerations of which we were guilty in 1920', thereby admitting that he had then expressed himself in an overdramatic and sometimes even offensive way. More seriously, he said that he should have paid more attention to the humanity of God.[3] For the Incarnation gives humanity a distinction and value that must be preserved and celebrated. He continued to insist that God held all humans and all religions to be sinful and faithless, and that man is not good. But he held that in Christ God had elected and even sanctified humanity, so that humans can become God's partners. There is thus a greater possibility of considering and supporting human talents and culture than he might earlier have done. Overall then, this change of emphasis is not a radical change of view about religion, but is primarily concerned with regarding humans not just as monsters, but as those who are called into partnership with God. This is what he had always thought, though it was largely hidden by the polemical tone of his earlier writings.

Nevertheless, Barth's views did develop in some respects, and in ways which are capable of further development, and it is only fair to take note of this. However, this is primarily a critique of what Barth thought and wrote about religion at one time, and left intact

---

[2] Karl Barth, *The Humanity of God*, trans. John Newton Thomas and Thomas Wieser (Louisville: John Knox Press, 1960 [1956]), p. 37.

[3] Ibid., p. 62.

in the *Church Dogmatics*. It is a critique, because I disagree almost entirely with what Barth said, and I will explain why this is. My critique is meant to give detailed attention to one topic that Barth treated early in his career, but not even to aim at assessing Barth's thought overall. Despite my profound disagreement, I have found Barth's work stimulating and helpful in formulating my own views on the topic. And I think it is important to have a detailed critique of at least one part of Barth's work, which deals with a topic within my own area of expertise.

He gives the general title of this section as 'The Revelation of God as the Sublimation of Religion'. This sounds like a neat and harmless phrase, which has a ring of profundity about it. Unfortunately, each of its three terms turns out to have a meaning which is surprising and provocative.

Barth's Idea of Sublimation

I will consider first the very unusual concept of 'sublimation'. This is a translation of the German *Aufhebung*, which was most clearly used by the philosopher Hegel to speak of the process of two apparently contradictory terms (for instance, 'being' and 'nothing') being cancelled and yet fulfilled in a 'higher' resolution (in this case, 'becoming'). It can also be used in reference to the alleged historical process in which an emphasis on one form of organisation led to a balancing emphasis on its opposite, and this in turn led to a higher synthesis (not Hegel's word) which at the same time cancelled both and yet preserved them in a higher form.

Hegel explains his use of the word as follows:

> At this point we should remember the double meaning of the German expression *aufheben*. On the one hand, we understand it to mean 'clear away' or 'cancel', and in that sense we say that a law or regulation is cancelled (*aufgehoben*). But the word also means 'to

preserve', and we say in this sense that something is well taken care of (*wohl aufgehoben*). This ambiguity in linguistic usage, through which the same word has a negative and a positive meaning, cannot be regarded as an accident nor yet as a reason to reproach language as if it was a source of confusion. We ought rather to recognise here the speculative spirit of our language, which transcends the 'either–or' of mere understanding.[4]

Examples in religion might be the way in which Jesus, in the sermon on the mount, at the same time could be said to have cancelled and yet fulfilled the inner meaning of the Torah. He cancelled it by saying, 'You have heard … but I say to you.' He fulfilled it by using it to refer not just to outward acts like murder, but to inner attitudes like anger or hatred.[5] He could also be said to have cancelled the idea of the Messiah, traditionally interpreted as the idea of a political liberator of Israel. This is perhaps why he told Peter not to tell people that he was the Messiah, though he apparently accepted Peter's attribution of the term to him.[6] For in another way he fulfilled the idea of Messiah, or Christ, by showing that he was a universal liberator of all humans from sin.

The Hegelian term used to be translated into English as 'sublation', a term which I myself have used, but it does not seem to have caught on. I intend to refer to the English translation by Garrett Green of this section of the *Church Dogmatics*, because I think this is the clearest English translation of the German text.[7] I shall throughout use Green's English translations of German terms. Green uses the term 'sublimation', and I do not object to this, even though,

[4] See G. W. F. Hegel, *Encyclopaedia Logic* (1830), trans. T. F. Geraets, H. S. Harris, and W. A. Suchting (Indianapolis: Hackett, 1991), annotation to para. 87, p. 154. This can also be found on the website hegel.net.
[5] Matthew 5, 21–4.
[6] Mark 8, 27–30.
[7] Karl Barth, *On Religion* (para. 17 of the *Church Dogmatics*, volume I, part 2), trans. Garrett Green (London: Bloomsbury, 2013); in-text references to page numbers are to this reissued edition.

as the Oxford English Dictionary confirms, the English word most often refers to various processes in chemistry or printing (so does 'sublation', of course). I will put in brackets in my text the page numbers of the passages I quote or refer to in the Bloomsbury edition translation. It is clearly a contentious and difficult concept in English, and Barth uses it in an unusual way in German. I shall hold that the sense in which Barth uses it is not helpful for an understanding of religion, and virtually eliminates the double meaning of cancellation and fulfilment which lies at the root of the word.

I find it odd that Barth should take this philosophical term from German Idealist thought to state his attitude to religion, when a large part of his argument is that theologians should not appeal to philosophy to justify their expositions of Christian faith. That, however, is just what he is doing in the very title of his writing on Christian attitudes to religion.

I do not suppose that Barth intends to use the idea of 'sublimation' in either a philosophical or a historical sense. Anyone who says that something 'cancels yet fulfils' religion needs to spell out just what is cancelled and what is fulfilled. In the Biblical cases I have referred to, what is cancelled is a purely external, behavioural interpretation of the Torah ('Do not kill'), and what is fulfilled (the 'full extent and meaning') is a reference to the inner thoughts of hatred that may occur. In my second example, what is cancelled is a political interpretation of Messiah (the victory of Israel), and what is fulfilled is the promise of liberation from sin for all.

2 | Barth's Theology of Religion

Barth's Idea of Religion

Continuing with my discussion of Barth's general heading to this part of the *Church Dogmatics*, I will address the question of what Barth thinks is cancelled in religion, and what is fulfilled. To do that, I will explore what Barth means by 'religion'. Right at the beginning, he states that it is 'the realm of attempts by man to justify and sanctify himself before a wilfully and arbitrarily devised image of God' (37). There are two parts to this definition, the attempt to justify oneself and the arbitrary construction of an image of God.

This is a very idiosyncratic definition of 'religion'. Why should Barth adopt it? I think the deepest reason lies in the general approach to theology that he is adopting, with which I am in some disagreement, and which he outlines at length in volume I, part 1 of the *Church Dogmatics*.

This is an approach which begins with the observation that no thinker begins with a blank sheet, without any preconceived opinions. Everyone has learned from their parents and society a set of general beliefs and attitudes. Some of these beliefs become systematised in such a way that they form totalising world-views. There are many very different world-views, some of them contradicting others, so they cannot all be true. Some thinkers hold that world-views cannot themselves be justified, because all the justifications they might give are contained within the world-view itself, and there is no universally agreed world-view in the light of which all the others can be assessed. Different basic world-views cannot therefore be compared. Religions, in particular, it is sometimes said, are different 'language-games', or forms of life,[1] with their own internal criteria of rationality, and though they can be criticised or expanded in various ways, they can never be compared with each other by some neutral rational criteria.

Some hold that they can only really be understood by insiders, and cannot be compared with other religions in any meaningful way.

Barth seems to have accepted that Christianity was like such a world-view, and Christian theology was a self-contained discipline that could not be justified by some neutral rational criteria, but stood as the systematic reflection on a faith that was directly revealed by God, not selected by human reasoning or choice. There was no need for apologetics as a necessary prelude to faith. Faith was directly given by the grace, the free choice, of God in Christ. As Barth puts it, revelation is 'the outpouring of the Holy Spirit ... the judging, but also reconciling presence of God' (36). Theology is the work of exploring this revelation in all its implications and presuppositions.

This definition can be clearly formulated and understood, whether one agrees with it or not. It gives, to use Bertrand Russell's formulation, knowledge by description of what revelation is.[2] One does not have to agree with it to have such understanding. But to be a Christian believer one must also have knowledge by acquaintance. That is, one must actually have some experience of the outpouring of the Spirit, and of the presence of a judging and reconciling God. That is a matter of receiving grace. One does not need any philosophical preparation for this, nor can one obtain it by one's own efforts. Faith is a pure gift of God, and one is entitled to use it as a

---

[1] These terms come from Ludwig Wittgenstein, *Philosophical Investigations*, trans. G. E. M. Anscombe (Oxford: Blackwell, 1958). It is doubtful, however, whether he would have approved of this use of them.

[2] See Bertrand Russell, *Knowledge by Acquaintance and Knowledge by Description*, Proceedings of the Aristotelian Society, Vol. XI (Oxford: Oxford University Press, 1910), pp. 108–28.

basis for theological thinking, for its God-given truth is more sure than any non-faith-based justification that might be offered for it.

Barth thereby distinguishes between religious knowledge by description and religious knowledge by acquaintance, though he does not use these terms, when he says that the Christian church (at least in its Reformed version) is 'the site' of God's revelation. He means that the church is not in itself the bearer of God's revelation. It may proclaim all the God-given beliefs, and yet, as a human religion, it may fail to live by them, and even undermine them in practice. But as proclaiming (perhaps among other things) the correct beliefs, it makes possible a life given and sustained by grace. It is this that makes Christianity the 'true religion'.

Barth thinks it possible to take the true religion as fundamental God-given knowledge which can have no other justification (no natural theology or proofs of God), and by which all human knowledge and activity can be judged. His discussion of religion is explicitly based on this foundation. For that reason, he distinguishes what he calls his 'theological' account of religion from accounts which he calls 'empirical', 'secular', or 'comparative'. He means by such non-theological accounts those which assume that no particular religion, or perhaps no religion, is true, or that regard Christianity as just one member of a more general category of 'religions', rather than as the religion by which all others must be judged.

This does, however, raise a major problem. For one's knowledge of God by acquaintance to be genuine, not illusory, one must have knowledge of God by description that is correct. But this is notoriously difficult to gain and to be sure of. Christian theology has from the beginning been marked by disputations, quite often violent ones. To mention some obvious ones, there are disputes about whether God is three 'persons' or three modes of being; whether Jesus is omniscient; whether God sends some to Hell; and whether good works are necessary to salvation. There are many others, and Barth has himself contributed to such debates.

In the case of the present debate, on the nature of religion, Barth proposes that religions, even Christian churches, that lack experience of the grace of Jesus Christ are all self-serving and wilful. But how does he know that? Many Christians, including me, would strongly resist this definition. It seems to impugn the sincerity and authenticity of many religions, and to restrict the grace of God to a relatively small group of people in an unacceptable way. It may be more adequate to think that many religions can be vehicles of God's grace.

I have no problem with regarding religions from a Christian point of view. But there are a number of Christian points of view, and I do not think all Christians would be able to agree with Barth's, even though they could understand it perfectly. For it is an exaggeration to say that religious views cannot be understood by those who do not believe them, or that they are not changeable and open to influence by others. Many Christians become atheists, and sometimes change back again. They understand both views perfectly well, while disbelieving one of them. I know Hindus who have become Christian, and I even know people who claim to be both Hindu and Christian (the Roman Catholic priest Raimon Panikkar being a notable example).[3]

It is perfectly possible to have a good understanding of more than one religion, even when disagreeing with many of their views – just as it is possible in politics for a conservative to understand very well what a socialist thinks, without being a socialist. Barth himself changed from a liberal view of Christian faith, and no longer believed it, but he understood it well enough. Many years of teaching theology have convinced me that it is possible for an atheist to give a better description of Christian beliefs than a committed Christian who firmly believes in Christ, but may be rather bad at theological thinking.

---

[3] See Raimon Panikkar, *The Unknown Christ of Hinduism* (Maryknoll: Orbis Books, 1981).

Christian writers may, like Barth, be much more creative in expanding or revising Christian doctrines, whereas non-Christians will have to be content with stating what various reputable Christians have taught. On the other hand, Christian writers may also come up with doctrines that are regarded by many of their fellow believers with horror, and have often later been regarded as heresies.

So there is every reason to be sceptical of Barth's claim that 'theological' accounts of religion will be essentially different from and better than what he terms 'secular' or 'empirical' accounts. In fact I intend to show by close attention to his text that the account he gives in *Church Dogmatics*, volume I, part 2, has harmful consequences for theology, in effect confining it to the discourse of an inward-looking and fideistic sect with little real interest in world religions or scientific and moral critiques of religion, and pretending that it has purely internal criteria of rationality to which more secular objections have no relevance.

A survey of the beliefs and practices of many human cultures shows that there are widespread human beliefs in a more valuable or ultimate spiritual reality, but many varied beliefs about how this reality should be described. Speaking of a judging and reconciling God, and an indwelling Spirit, as Christians do, is just one of these descriptions. It is unjustifiable to ignore different descriptions in a discussion about 'the world of human religion', which Barth must be intending to give if he is to provide a Christian theology of religion. It suggests that only one set of descriptions is correct, and even if that is true, how could one know that without investigating others?

I applaud Barth for his commitment to the Lordship of Christ and his opposition to allying Christian faith with totalitarian or repressive political ends. But, in an age when it is important to build up understanding of other cultures and their belief systems, Barth's method of regarding all world religions as wilful and arbitrary seems alienating and harmful.

More importantly, it seems in marked tension with believing that God is a being of unlimited and universal mercy and love, which is widely thought to be the teaching of Jesus. If God's mercy is unlimited, it might seem that God's grace would be given in some way to all cultures. If so, it is important to explore how this could be, and to understand why so many different views of an alleged spiritual reality have come to exist. Barth's 'theological' method of regarding all religions as wilful and arbitrary seems extremely unhelpful. It is not obvious that Christian revelation compels such a conclusion. It might be more appropriate to see if there is something more positive to be said about religions from within a properly Christian theology. That is one thing this book is intended to show.

One would certainly have to investigate with care whether non-Christian faiths are 'abominated by God', or whether they may show signs of God's love and grace. It would not be enough to ignore them completely.

I do not have a problem with seeing that religious believers can describe other belief systems while being loyal to their own revelation, which in the Christian case is what I think Barth means by giving a properly 'theological' account. But we must be very careful to describe such systems and religions accurately and sensitively, and try to see what indications, if any, can be seen in them of God's presence and activity.

This is what a theological account, on Barth's own terms, requires. Unfortunately, although Barth gives brief accounts of some forms of Buddhism and Hinduism, and thus is clearly dealing not just with Christianity, but with world religions as a whole, there are many internal problems of consistency, coherence, and sectarian bias in his treatment of religion, as I endeavour to show.

The Limited Scope of Barth's Idea of Religion

For a start, although he defines religion as concerned with imaginary and wilful ideas of God, many religions (Buddhism is the obvious example) do not particularly concern themselves with ideas of God at all. They obviously have no concern to justify themselves before a God in whom they do not believe, and would have no idea of what it means to sanctify themselves before such an imaginary figure.

So Barth, in this definition, is only concerned with the group of religions which are theistic, which see a need to 'justify' themselves (declare themselves innocent of offence?), and which care about being sanctified ('made holy') by or before God. Such religions have a God who assesses their conduct, probably finds them guilty, and maybe then has a way of reconciling them to God.

This sounds as though it is already confined to some versions of Christianity. Jews and Muslims, for example, do not generally consider themselves morally guilty before God, even in the best actions they perform, and before they have done anything. Such a thing sounds like a doctrine of total depravity, which is characteristic of some Protestant theologies. The doctrine holds that humans have been so depraved by the 'fall' of the first humans from grace that they can no longer do anything which will make them good (righteous) enough to be acceptable to God. They therefore stand in need of some saviour-figure who can reconcile them to God. Jews and Muslims typically consider that humans are mixtures of good and bad, and if they do their best to obey God, that is all that can be required of them. They have no notion of 'original guilt', and no notion of 'original sin', seen as a total inability to please God, which is somehow inherited from Adam and Eve.[4] They can accept that humans find it very difficult to do what is right, and that they often lack any sense of the presence of God. Jews might also say that many of the sufferings of human life are the results of a 'fall', a turning from God and towards egoistic and harmful behaviour that occurred in the earliest days of the human race. But there is no notion of personal guilt for something that they themselves did not do. Humans may need divine help to do what is right and to

---

[4] The reader can confirm this by looking up 'original sin' on any reputable Jewish or Muslim website.

come to know God, but that help will be given by God as a result of prayer and trust in God. There is no need of some figure who suffers in order to pay for their sin. Indeed, such an idea may even seem ludicrous to them.

Jews and Muslims are, like Christians, concerned with righteousness, with justice and compassion. They do recognise that humans continually fail to live up to their moral ideals. They do believe that God needs to forgive them and help them to be more just and compassionate, and that God will do so. They are not seeking to justify themselves, but they think that God will justify them if they turn to God in trust and obedience.

There may, from a Christian point of view, be something lacking if there is no idea of God sharing in the human condition, but there is no lack of trust in God, and there is no attempt at self-justification. Such accusations would be rejected by most Jews and Muslims, and so the accusations cannot be seen to show real understanding of Jewish and Muslim belief. They are only, sad to say, repetitions of the calumnies that Christians have made of Judaism and Islam throughout most of history. It is sad to see Barth supporting them, when I am sure that he had no intention of doing so.

So Barth seems to be only considering religions with a morally judging God who might nevertheless provide some sort of help to overcome their moral failures. That may already seem a very paradoxical view of God. We might understand that there could be a God who judged human lives in the light of very high moral standards. But if, because of some inherited tendency in their make-up, they actually could not meet those standards, we might think that even a moderately reasonable God would not condemn people for what they could not help. If a theologian goes on to say that God does condemn everyone, but then forgives them, this may well seem totally unreasonable. It would be more just to say that, when people cannot meet very high moral standards, through no personal fault of their own, then this is a mitigating circumstance which will make total condemnation inappropriate. People should only be condemned for what they did that was wrong, but that they need not have done, though they knew it was wrong. That is a first principle of justice, in most legal systems. There will be punishments for evil, but the punishments will be proportioned to the seriousness of the crime, and they will probably be finite.

Jews, in fact, may not believe in any sort of afterlife in which punishments could take place – the Sadducees at the time of Jesus took this view, and many Jews today would do so too. For them, punishments would probably take the form of disastrous consequences for the family or society of which the wrongdoer was part. Muslims almost all believe in a life after death, and in a Hell where punishments take place. But they passionately believe that repentance and faith will mitigate those punishments, and many think that most punishments will be finite, and can be relieved by, for example, the intercession of the Prophet.[5]

Divine forgiveness is an important feature of both Judaism and Islam, but it is a general principle of justice that a judge should not just forgive people because he feels like it, even though they deserve condemnation and punishment. Barth calls such forgiveness 'grace', and applauds the thought that forgiveness is given freely and out of divine love and compassion. But the fact is that, however compassionate forgiveness without regard to the nature or action of wrongdoers may be, it would seem to many people to be simply unjust. Forgiveness is always difficult, but is usually only possible if the wrongdoers repent and are prepared to do something to make amends, where such a thing is possible. So in Judaism and Islam God will forgive the truly penitent, if they are prepared to act in a way that shows a genuine desire to act righteously, and if they turn to God in faith.

---

[5] There are Hadiths which say as much, and the Qur'an 7, 29 – 'soon will thy Lord raise thee to a station of praise and glory' – is interpreted by Islamic scholars to be addressed to the Prophet, and means that he will successfully intercede for the release from Hell of many on Judgment Day.

The claim that Barth seems to make, that God at the same time both totally condemns all human acts, however good they may seem, and totally forgives them, without regard to the merit or actions of the wrongdoers, can seem irrational and unjust. The thought that this is possible because God, in human form, pays the penalty for sin (for something God did not do) is no help. Many people, not only Jews and Muslims, would say that only the wrongdoer can pay the penalty for wrongdoing. If God is all-powerful and compassionate, it would be better and easier for God just to forgive the wrongdoing anyway, and ignore the penalty.

That is how it would seem to a Jew or Muslim, and I think it has to be said that their objections are not unreasonable, and in no way show a desire for self-justification. It is still God who forgives, but God forgives the moral failures of humans insofar as they repent and desire to make amends. And God, after perhaps some form of punishment for their misdoings, makes it possible for them to achieve conscious fellowship with the divine by giving them divine help.

Obviously Christians would not completely agree with Jewish and Muslim accounts. But they should also say that such accounts have nothing to do with self-justification or rejection of God. They give a rather different account of God's nature and the nature of judgment and forgiveness. For Christians, it may seem to be an inadequate, and to that extent wrong, account. But it is not wholly wrong, and it is surely not, as Barth puts it, an abomination to God. I would go so far as to say that it is an account which puts genuine question marks to some Christian accounts of the matter, and it is an honest attempt to worship God in sincerity and truth.

I think that what Christians can stress is an insistence that God is a God of love, and so one with whom a relationship of love can be established; a belief that God can be imaged in a human life which gives this love a human face; a perception that human sin causes God to share in human suffering; a faith that the Spirit of Christ is given to humans in the community of the church; and a vision of the goal of the cosmos as a loving and creative union in Christ. Jews and Muslims would not put it like this. But they could say that God is loving and compassionate; that God reveals a way to turn to God; that God promises that a community of peace and justice is the goal of human existence; and that this goal will, by God's power, be realised, whether in this world or beyond it.

In light of this, it seems almost self-contradictory of Barth to say that the Jewish and Muslim ideas of God are 'wilful and arbitrary'. Moreover, the Jewish idea of God as a moral creator who makes an unbreakable covenant with the Jews is recorded in a book which Christians call 'the Old Testament', so the revelation of the Torah to Jews must be at least part of the revelation of God to Christians. Muslims inherit this tradition of divine revelation and covenant, though they universalise God's covenant to the whole human race. So theirs must be the same God too, even if slightly different things are said about God. It follows that either the Christian idea of God is wilful and arbitrary too, or that Jewish and Muslim ideas of God, together with the God of other Abrahamic religions, are on the whole correct.

Differences will remain, just as differences remain among various Christian traditions. Religions will be misused to support tyrannical political powers and to encourage violence and hatred. But it is better to look for the elements which promote friendship and a sense of sharing in a spiritual quest for goodness and well-being in the world, rather than to suggest that all religions are vain quests for self-justification and barriers to divine revelation.

Buddhism

In thinking about religion, I have so far only mentioned religions that originated in the Eastern Mediterranean, and form what is often called the Abrahamic tradition. But there are many other types of religion in the world, and many of them are so unlike Christianity that the question of self-justification scarcely even arises. It is impossible to deal with them all, and in a book of this nature one cannot give a fully adequate account of any world religion. But it is important to raise the question of whether all the major world religions (oddly, including Christianity) are abominated by God, as Barth claims. I will aim to give necessarily rather general accounts, which will be enough to suggest that there are many more positive things to be said about many religions than Barth allows.[6] I will refer in each case to one or two major strands of the traditions I discuss, and I will begin by choosing two which Barth mentions, Buddhism and Hinduism.

Buddhism in particular can look very unlike Christianity, and some versions of it can seem to have nothing in common with Christian faith. But the situation is very complex. There are many groups which practise a union of Buddhist and Christian beliefs and meditation techniques, and it is not too difficult to find affinities between them.[7]

There is obviously no question of seeking to justify oneself before a personal creator God, since there is no such God in the Buddhist way. But there is a central search for holiness, or liberation from egoism and from the 'three fires' of hatred, greed, and ignorance. Christians might speak of holiness as full obedience to the moral law, devotion to a personal God, and being filled with Christ's love and the power of the divine Spirit. Buddhists are not going to use such terms. But the Eightfold Path, which is the heart of Buddhist practice, involves commitment to a morality of compassion for all beings which is much greater and wider than much traditional Christian practice. Christians tend to speak of love for other human beings, but have often been insensitive to the welfare

---

[6] I have given much fuller accounts of Buddhism and Hinduism in a five-volume series, each headed *Religion and …* (four with Oxford University Press 1994–2000, and the fifth volume with SCM, 2008). A one-volume account is in my *Images of Eternity* (London: Darton, Longman, Todd, 1987), later retitled as *Concepts of God* (London: Oneworld, 1998).

[7] See the essays in Gavin D'Costa and Ross Thompson, eds., *Buddhist–Christian Dual Belonging* (Farnham: Ashgate, 2016).

of animals. Christians have even been accused of thinking that all other beings exist for the sake of humans, and that animals and the earth itself can be used in any way at all if it promotes human interests. Thomas Aquinas wrote, 'The whole of material nature exists for man',[8] and some have taken this to mean that humans can treat animals as they wish. This is not wholly fair – St Francis did, after all, exist, and the first chapters of Genesis begin with the story of humans tending and caring for the Garden of Eden.[9] But it is true that compassion for all beings certainly includes concern for the welfare of animals, and also for the flourishing of the environment and the whole planet. Buddhism arguably has a better record than Christianity in this regard.

In Buddhism there is no God who commands obedience to divine law and judges humans by that law. But there is a cosmic law of karma, according to which all thoughts and actions have consequences for good or ill. That law is interpreted in many ways, but it is certainly not thought of as a purely human invention or convention. It is more like a law of nature, ensuring that any form of selfish desire, in either thought or action, will generate suffering. Any thought or action of compassion will generate happiness or contentment. To use a rather crude example, if I hate another person, that hatred will cause unhappiness both in myself and in others, as I interact with them.

The goal of Buddhist practice is to escape suffering or discontent. To do this I have to eliminate such things as hatred, and practice thoughts and acts of compassion and loving-kindness. Some sceptics about Buddhism have said that this is a selfish goal, since it is aimed at personal happiness. But that is a real misunderstanding. The goal is to eliminate suffering from the world, not just from oneself.

[8] Thomas Aquinas, *The Light of Nature* (Bedford, NH: Sophia Institute Press, 1991), sect. 148.
[9] Genesis 2, 15.

The truth is that a central doctrine of Buddhism is the doctrine of anatta or 'no-self'. There is no continuing or immortal self. A person is a flowing succession of thoughts, feelings, perceptions, and intentions. They are causally linked, each one existing only for an instant, and causing another to arise, either in the same or in another flow. There is only the flow. There is nothing permanent underlying the flow. All is transient. The notion of 'I', as a continuing entity, is an illusion.

We say in ordinary life that persons continue to exist from being babies until they die. But a Buddhist would say that the person who dies is different from the baby he or she used to be. It is no doubt part of the same flow of perceptions, but every element of that flow has changed innumerable times. Once you see this, you see that egoism is impossible. What I think of as my future self is a different section of a constant flow. I am a different person every day, even every second, as the flow which I call 'me' continues.

My egoistic thoughts, intended for the good of a future me, in fact, by the law of karma, generate unsatisfactory feelings in some future flow. But that is not 'me'. It is just some part of a sentient flow. So my thoughts and acts do affect the future, by changing the flow of experiences in some future being.

That is why there is a Buddhist saying that we neither live after death, nor do we not live after death.[10] Something continues after my body dies, but it is not a continuing 'I'. It is no longer me. The Buddhist teaching is not that I should be unselfish. It is that I am not a self – so I cannot be selfish. Buddhists might in fact accuse Christianity of being a form of long-term prudence. A concern for personal salvation, and for the endless existence of my continuing self, can sound rather self-interested. Of course Christians might reply that their concern is not for the individual self, but for the continuing selves of all humans. Those whose lives have been

[10] See Majjhima-Nikaya, I, Discourse 4, in David Evans, trans., *Discourses of Gautama Buddha* (London: Janus, 1992), p. 27.

curtailed by illness and marked by years of slavery will be able to find fulfilment and happiness in a continued life beyond death. Such a concern for others cannot be called selfish. But one can see the Buddhist argument that if there is no continuing self to be interested in, that is a sure way to combat self-interest.

This argument could continue, but what is clear is that the Buddhist view of what a human being essentially is will be very different from a Christian one. Most traditional Buddhists would not have personal immortality as an ultimate goal. They would look for liberation from samsara, the round of rebirths in a world of suffering. They seek a fading away of the sense of a personal self, and entrance into a supra-personal state of nirvana, a state which is indescribable, but is neither a continuation of some finite personality nor a simple annihilation of existence.

Since these beliefs about human nature and about the ultimate goal of existence are so very different in most forms of Buddhism and of Christianity, at least one of them must be false, and perhaps both of them are. But what Barth seems to be saying is that it is not just a question of which is false. It is a question of whether one is a damnable form of rebellion against divine truth, and the other is the only one which genuinely promises liberation from sin and a final fulfilment of human life.

That is an opposition which simply does not exist in reality. Buddhists would not damn or condemn the honest holding of a false belief. They would have compassion for those who, in their opinion, are deluded about the nature of human existence and about the way to end suffering. But they would believe that there will be many lives in which people can come to learn the truth. Damnation is temporary (though there are said to be as many as eight Hells), and is only for those who are attached to self-regarding and other-harming ways of life. Theoretical questions about such things are discouraged, and what matters is the lessening of self-regard and harmful action, and the attainment of mindfulness, or freedom from passion. There is no rebellion against divine truth, since the existence of a God is regarded as a purely speculative question which has few, if any, implications for how the way of non-attachment can be effectively pursued.

I think Christians have much to learn from this prioritising of how one lives and how one overcomes attachments to desire over theoretical questions about whether there is a God. Many Christians are seeking to learn from Buddhists, and Buddhist techniques of meditation and mindfulness are now being practised by some Christians. They obviously do not think that Buddhism is a damnable and faithless rebellion against God. It would be more accurate to say that the question of God is simply not of great interest to Buddhists. They would regard the interminable, and often violent, arguments between Christians about such things as how God could become man, or whether God is three or one, or whether people are saved by works or by faith, as unresolvable and almost wholly irrelevant. What matters is whether one lives selflessly and dispassionately, and without hatred, greed, and ignorance.

Revelation and Buddhism

But, Christians may say, if God is of little interest to Buddhists, how can their religion be considered a form of divine revelation? There is no divine revelation in many of the more traditional forms of Buddhism, in the sense of gods speaking or appearing to human beings. Buddhism is a human search for truth. It is committed, however, to a view that thoughts, perceptions, and feelings are the basis of all knowledge and of reality itself. The idea of materialism, that ultimately there is nothing but physical objects in space-time, is foreign to Buddhism. The law of karma subordinates the laws of physics to a law of moral causality – where thoughts cause suffering or bliss. This causality is not apparent, or to be blunt, is not present, in the physical world, and so it must be taken to operate in other realms, or over many lives (rebirth). There must also be a more basic and non-physical form of cosmic order (in the tradition, there are also many Heavens). The goal of enlightenment is also a non-material goal, which is believed to liberate humans from the physical world, and transform them in a non-physical or spiritual reality.

This may sound more like a philosophy than a religion, and for that reason some writers refuse to call it a religion. But it is not just a philosophy, based on reasoning and logic. It is based on meditative experience, and the Buddha, the enlightened one, is believed to have passed beyond physical existence and beyond suffering and rebirth, and to have shown the way to others. It has an authority, based on the experience of one who has overcome disordered desire and suffering. And it has a spiritual practice, a discipline of meditation and moral striving, which leads to the end of suffering.

This is a search for spiritual truth and human fulfilment, inspired by people believed to be enlightened, who have discerned the nature of reality, and conquered self-centred desire.

From a Christian viewpoint, is that search self-justificatory? Is it damnable? Or is it a genuine seeking for a reality and a way of life which will alleviate the unsatisfactory nature of human existence? It seems both ignorant and abusive to deny the sincerity of this spiritual search. It is also hard to believe that it is a way that has completely failed.

What it claims to have discovered, through personal discipline and experience, is that human life is disordered because of undue attachment to transient and unsatisfactory things. This is very like what Christians would call a sense of sin. It has discovered that the overcoming of attachment and the arising of universal compassion brings liberation from this human condition. This is very like what Christians call following the way of the cross, in self-giving love and compassion, in order to experience the way of resurrection, in a new and freer life. Buddhists believe it is possible to transcend this physical and embodied life, and pass into a greater realm beyond, which has the nature of intelligence and bliss, but is not further describable in any human language. This is very like what Christian mystics have said about the possibility of eternal life.

There is no sense of a personal God, or of the power of grace, or of the need for forgiveness. Those things are not spoken of in that way. There is, however, a sense of a supreme reality beyond the physical, into which an enlightened person can enter, in a life beyond suffering and ignorance. There is a sense of a calling to renounce the world, and follow a difficult path to spiritual perfection, and hopefully towards increasing insight into the bliss of the liberated state. And there is a sense of a gradual overcoming of greed, hatred, and ignorance as one turns from attachment.

This may not be enough for Christians, who wish for a loving relation to God, experience of the Spirit helping their endeavours, and forgiveness for their continuing moral failures. But that is no reason to condemn the Buddhist religion. Christians want to speak of a personal God who actively relates to us, and brings about a loving communion in which we can participate. Traditional Buddhists speak rather of a human search for a liberating spiritual experience. It may be the case that both approaches are needed to gain a fuller insight into the human condition.

In Christian tradition, there are many who insist on an apophatic understanding of God, in which every positive attribute is denied of the divine being itself. Even for Aquinas, God is *esse ipsem esse per se subsistens*, 'self-subsistent being itself', unchanging and simple and impassible.[11] This does not sound like saying that God is some sort of person, or is a grossly magnified human-like being. Is it so clear that the state of liberation in Buddhism is completely different from union with a reality which cannot in any way be changed by that union, and which can never be literally described or fully understood?

I understand that Barth would be suspicious of any monastic practice of asceticism and meditation, regarding it as part of

---

[11] Thomas Aquinas, *Summa Theologiae*, Prima Pars, various translators (London: Blackfriars, 1966), 1a, 4, 2.

a 'religion of works', and so opposed to salvation by faith alone. In doing so, he would be condemning many orthodox Christians, which is rather strange for a theologian. Yet Barth, as will be noted in due course, holds that good works are to be pursued as a discipline, though only after and in response to the prevenient forgiveness and grace of God.

Buddhists would not speak of the prevenient grace of God. They might indeed stress that liberation is to be obtained by personal effort, by what is often called 'own-power'. However, if forgiveness is regarded as a declaration of freedom from penalty, then Buddhists can be freed from the penal consequences of their harmful actions by the law of karma. It is not accurate to say that they free themselves by what is completely within their own power. For their power is given to them with their existence; it is not generated by them alone. And it is the karmic law which ordains that the exercise of their powers will cause good or bad effects, which ensures that specific actions will eliminate 'bad karma', or freedom from penalty for harmful acts. Liberation is produced by effort; but that it does so is not of their making. It is part of the objective nature of things, part of the moral ordering of reality. There is not so much difference between saying that God forgives freely, but only sanctifies when creatures obey God's laws, and saying that the bad effects of harmful actions are cancelled when persons obey the moral laws of the universe.

There is, it is true, no sense of a personal God who forgives and establishes a personal relationship with humans. But there is a sense of an objective moral order which makes possible actions freeing humans from suffering, and is capable of leading them to a perfected state. Even that perfected state, nirvana, is not of their own making, but is part of the nature of things, and the ultimate goal of spiritual life. If there is a moral order in the universe, which ordains that goodness and compassion are to be pursued, and that there is a goal beyond suffering which is possible of attainment by all, how different is that from saying that there is a God who ordains such things?

There are differences, obviously, and I do not want to deny them. I only want to suggest that making one simple contrast between Buddhism and Christianity is misleading. There are many different strands in each 'religion'. Many Christians, including the most orthodox, do not view God as a person or even as a personal being. They regard the moral law as not arbitrarily commanded by God, but as a necessary part of the ultimate nature of things, perhaps of the divine nature itself. And they regard eternal life not as a continuation of this life, but as a wholly different and changeless order of being that we cannot now imagine.[12] That is pretty near to the Buddhist view.

Many Buddhists do not take the rather severe view of Hinayana Buddhism to which I have mostly referred. They have a place for devotion to gods and Bodhisattvas, beings in Heaven who have delayed their own liberation in order to help their devotees on earth. Barth himself makes remarks about the Japanese Buddhist school, Jodo-Shin-Shu, which talks of entry to the Western Paradise by a simple declaration of faith and devotion to Amida Buddha, who has created that Paradise. This, Barth says, comes very close to Christianity indeed. I shall discuss this later, but the fact is that Barth rejects this movement just because it does not speak of Jesus Christ. He apparently does not consider, at least in this stage in what he wrote, the possibility that the grace of God could be given in more than one way, even if, as Christians think, Jesus is a uniquely normative expression of grace.

The fact is that virtually all religions have adherents who regard their faith as the only acceptable one, so that all others should be eliminated. Barth is not in favour of elimination, but he does think Protestant Christianity is the only acceptable faith. That does seem a rather dangerous view in the modern world, where believers in non-Christian faiths are passionately committed to them, and it seems to limit God's grace in a very severe way.

---

[12] I take such a view in *Christianity: A Beginner's Guide* (London: Oneworld, 2000).

An alternative view is to see one's own religious way as one spiritual path among others. Some doctrines of many faiths may be regarded as false. But some doctrines and practices may be seen as having affinities to one's own, even stressing insights that are not present in one's own tradition. Many religions may be seen as being honest attempts at seeking the truth about spiritual reality and establishing positive relations with it, in a world where certainty is hard to attain, and differences might actually stimulate and increase understanding.

Hinduism

There is one religious tradition that seems to me to have a much greater positive affinity with Christianity. It is one that Barth also refers to, though he is very dismissive of it, as we shall see. It is the tradition of devotion to Vishnu or to his eighth avatar, Krishna, which is often influenced by the teachings of Ramanuja, the twelfth-century Vedantin.[13] It is impossible to speak of Hinduism as one religion, as within it there are a great many different *sampradaya*, or what might be called sects. One important part of the Hindu tradition is Vedanta, which means a meditation on the Vedas, early sacred writings, but is mostly based on the Upanishads. There are many different schools of Vedanta, ranging from the view of an early theologian, Sankara, that there is only one spiritual reality, Brahman, of which all things are parts, to Madhva's defence of a dualism of spirit and matter, which both together form Brahman. This diversity of interpretations is a central feature of what is called Hinduism, and it confirms the opinion that the internal diversity of each religion is often at least as great as the diversity of what we call 'religions'. That is a major reason for refusing to divide the 'world religions' into separate blocks of beliefs and practices which have clear and

---

[13] An excellent introduction to Ramanuja is: Julius Lipner, *'The Face of Truth'* (New York: State University of New York Press, 1986). See also my *Concepts of God*, chapter 2.

unchanging boundaries. That will in turn throw doubt on Barth's practice of calling all religions faithless except for one version of Christianity, which can be clearly distinguished and separated from all the others by being the only vehicle of the grace of God.

Ramanuja is one of the major theologians of India, and has influenced millions of devotees. It is well known that Sankara held that the phrase *Tat tvam asi* ('Thus are you', or, as it is often more archaically expressed in English, 'Thou art that'), which is central to Vedantic teaching, means that you and all things are identical with Brahman. Brahman is a reality of consciousness, intelligence, and bliss, and it is the only reality. Yet it appears in illusory form as a physical universe of many things, including many gods and intelligent souls, some of whom are human. For Sankara, all these forms are illusory, or like dream images, and the truth lies in seeing through the illusion, and apprehending the unity of the one Self which has taken many illusory forms. This view is known as Advaita, non-duality, for reality is one, and all the things and people we know are illusory appearances.

Ramanuja takes a very different interpretation of the same phrase, *Tat tvam asi*. He too holds that reality is one, and that all things, the universe and all intelligent souls, are parts of that one reality. Yet the universe and finite souls are not just illusions. They are real. But they are real as parts of Brahman. One of his most distinctive doctrines is that the universe is 'the body of Brahman'.[14] Parts of the body are real, but they are not distinct from the body.

This may seem to conflict with a typical Christian view that the created universe is not part of God. God creates distinct individuals, and some of those individuals – namely, human beings – have sinned. So they are definitively not parts of God, who cannot sin. As always in religion, it seems, there exist more rigid and more flexible interpretations of these different views. The rigid interpretations

---

[14] Ramanuja, *The Vedanta Sutras*, trans. George Thibaut, in *Sacred Books of the East*, Vol. XLVIII, ed. Max Muller (New Delhi: Motilal Banarsidass, 1962), p. 95.

say that humans are, on the one hand, completely identical with Brahman, the supreme Self, or on the other hand that they are completely separated from it. More flexible interpretations focus on the various possible meaning of the phrase 'is part of God'. It might not mean total identity, associated with Sankara, and it might not mean total dissimilarity, a view associated with Madhva.

Ramanuja's view is a more flexible one. There is only one reality, but it has distinct parts. An analogy of Ramanuja's view might be that a cell is part of my body, but not strictly identical with it. This catches the sense that the physical universe and the many intelligent souls could not exist and be what they are apart from the supreme Self. It also implies that souls, being intelligent and creative, have the same nature as the supreme Self, and can share in the most intimate communion with the supreme Self.

Put like this, the difference between Vedantin and Christian views is not so great. Human souls have individual creativity, and they have sinned or fallen into self-centred ignorance and become estranged from communion with the Self of all. It is as if some cells of the body have become diseased. But they can be reconciled and re-establish such communion. That is their true nature, and its realisation is their true goal. After all, the Christian Scriptures say that all things will be united 'in Christ',[15] that the church is 'the body of Christ',[16] and that 'in God we live and move and have our being'.[17] Since Christ is the divine being, this implies that souls can become parts of the divine being, that at least some created souls are already parts of the divine being, and that the world is in some sense part of God.

Traditional Christians in the West (the Latin tradition) have been hesitant to take talk of being 'the body of Christ' seriously. The more Idealist philosophy of much Upanishadic thought suggests

[15] Ephesians 1, 10.
[16] 1 Corinthians 12, 27.
[17] Acts 17, 28.

the idea that all things are parts of the divine, and that God is not just other and apart from the cosmos. In modern philosophy, such a view is sometimes called 'panentheism' (that the cosmos is part of God, but God is more than the cosmos).[18] To see human beings as sharers in the divine nature, as indeed some parts of the New Testament suggest,[19] seems to me a more positive way of looking at them than seeing them as miserable worms and damned sinners.

If we are prepared to take a flexible interpretation of beliefs, it becomes much more difficult to oppose religious doctrines to each other as rigid oppositions. The use of the term 'sublation' or 'sublimation' can be usefully employed to turn rigid oppositions (we are parts of God, or we are not) into a mediating synthesis (we are, or can be and should be, in close union with God, without losing our individual identities). Barth uses the term sublimation of one religion, but does not see that it could usefully qualify the oppositions between different religions. It will not resolve all differences into one vague and confused mess, but it could lessen the hostility different religions could feel for one another if they felt each was just being derided as false or even as idolatrous by the other. Regrettably, this opposition and hostility is what Barth seems to be attributing to all religions, since he does not use his concept of sublimation to seek mediating interpretations which might, if not achieving agreement, at least negate the necessity of hostile oppositions.

Ramanuja disagrees with Sankara by denying that there is such a thing as Nirguna Brahman – the supreme reality in itself without qualities, which is the only true reality. Sankara's is an almost totally apophatic view of the ultimately real. It holds that there are no distinct properties that the supreme Self has; it is wholly 'simple' (non-complex). Ramanuja rejects this view, since that of which nothing can be said cannot even be said to exist, which sounds very odd,

---

[18] The term was originated by the German philosopher Karl Krause in 1828 to describe the views of Hegel.

[19] 2 Peter 1, 4.

since we are presumably referring to it. Instead, he says, the supreme Self has the qualities which belong to a perfect consciousness – wisdom, bliss, power, and all other personal perfections. It can therefore be regarded as a personal being, and can be revered and loved.[20]

The concept of sublimation can be employed to reject a total opposition between an unknowable Reality and an anthropomorphic notion of God as a person. The mediating synthesis would then be a reality beyond the possibility of literal human description in its essential nature, yet truly describable as perfectly wise and loving in relation to finite beings. This idea reflects the dialectic within Christian theology between the unknowable and the personal God, and sublimation transforms an oppositional dispute into a polarity of images which are both needed to grasp the nature of the Supreme.

This could easily be seen as an instance of the dialectical theology for which Barth is famous. The idea of the Absolute Self as truly relating in love and personal interaction with human beings is actually more unambiguously formulated in Ramanuja than it has been in much traditional Christian theology. For many Christian theologians, the idea of God has been deeply influenced by Aristotle, who held that a perfect being would have to be changeless and simple. Strange though it may seem, such theologians have then held that God loves us, becomes incarnate, answers our prayers, and even includes us in the divine life, without ever changing or being affected by our existence in any way. That is not very different from Sankara's view that the world, though real on its own level, is at best a half-real realm of appearances which has no effect on the ultimately real. In that case, to know the Real we would have to know the Unchanging, of which we ourselves are only transitory and even illusory appearances.

Ramanuja's view is rather different. He sees the Real as a loving, changing, relational, complex Lord. That is nearer the heart

---

[20] Ramanuja, *Vedanta Sutras*, p. 4.

of the Biblical tradition, and also nearer to Christianity than 'the God of the philosophers' scathingly mentioned by Blaise Pascal.[21] It is certainly not an arbitrary or wilful idea which is opposed to the 'real' God of Christian faith. Despite what Barth says about the banality of Hindu thought, Ramanuja's is in fact a sophisticated and thoughtful exploration of the nature of the supreme being.

The similarity to Christian views is even closer than that. Christians speak of God present within the heart (the Holy Spirit), as a particular person who is the image of the Eternal (the Son), and as a cosmic all-including being of consciousness, wisdom, and bliss (the Father). That is echoed in Ramanuja by the ideas of the 'self within', Krishna as the personal face of the supreme reality, and the cosmos as the 'body of the Lord'.

I am not suggesting that these are the same ideas in different dress, but that there are significant affinities between these two spiritual paths. Christians today often feel that in traditional Christian theology not enough emphasis has been given to the work of the Spirit, and I think that encounter with Indian spiritualities, even when they have been rather transfigured by Western ideas, has helped to generate within Christianity a greater stress on the 'God within'.[22]

Devotion in Hinduism and Christianity

Ramanuja was a Sri Vaishnavite, a devotee of the god Vishnu, and his work is a main doctrinal resource of the bhakti tradition in Hinduism. That is a richly devotional tradition, which holds that the goal of human existence is the passionate love of God and of course, therefore, of all that God has created. It is not held that devotion

---

[21] See the 'Memorial', found sewn into the French mathematician and philosopher Blaise Pascal's clothing after his death, recording a vision that occurred on 23 November 1654.

[22] For some years I was chair of the governors of the Oxford Centre for Hindu Studies, and I found a fascinating interplay between the 'Western' philosophies of Idealism and the 'Eastern' philosophical traditions of Vedanta.

is the only way to God, but it is a way to which many feel called, a particular human vocation. This resonates with the Christian way of devotion to Jesus, who is seen as the human face of God. Bhakti clearly requires faith in the Supreme Lord, trust in his ways, and obedience to his will.

Ramanuja wrote an influential commentary on the Indian devotional work the Bhagavadgita, the Song of the Lord. That work celebrates the love of Krishna, an avatar or earthly manifestation of Vishnu. Many Indian religious communities are devoted to Krishna or Vishnu, and Ramanuja is a major theologian for those traditions. Though there are differences between the idea of an avatar, who is the Lord appearing as a human, and the idea of Incarnation in Christianity, they both believe that the Supreme Lord can appear in human form, and is a proper object of devotion and loyalty.

There are, naturally, other differences between the Hindu and Christian traditions. There is little or no idea of a suffering God in Vaishnava thought, since the Lord is perfect in bliss.[23] And there is no thought of Krishna as a sacrifice for sin, since as the Lord he is beyond suffering. Christians generally think that God shares in the sufferings of creation, and that a divine saviour gives his life to liberate humans from evil and suffering. This is not a major element in Vaishnavism, any more than it is in Islam.

There is no doubt, however, that Vishnu promises his devotees a joyful and loving relation in the spiritual realm, and that Krishna came to save people from the hardships of this world. Devotion to Krishna will bring them close to him, and it is his love which saves them from evil.[24]

This may be a case where sublimation can play a part in relating religions more sympathetically to each other, as the Vaishnava emphasis on the joy and love of relationship with a playful and mischievous

---

[23] Ramanuja, *Vedanta Sutras*, p. 610.
[24] 'I promise you will come to me, because you are to me so dear', *Bhagavad Gita*, 18, 65, trans. Geoffrey Parrinder (London: Sheldon, 1974), p. 101.

avatar mitigates the sometimes rather sado-masochistic wallowing in the blood of a dying Christ on the cross that is prominent in much Western art and devotion. Whether this is possible or not, it is not hard to see bhakti as an authentic spiritual path to sanctification, and to see its idea of God as a revelation of the divine love. It is hard to see it in Barth's terms as a faithless construction of little worth.

I suppose it is the seeming polytheism of Hinduism which most annoyed Barth. It cannot be denied that there have been hostilities between devotees of different gods, which means that Hinduism is not as peaceful and tolerant as some Western admirers have thought. But in principle the gods are more like Christian angels or saints than they are like the Christian God. Devotees can choose gods that appeal to them – but when they do that, it is usually said to be because they feel the god 'call' to them. It is not at all a matter of random selection. It is a response to a spiritual reality which calls them.

For theologians like Ramanuja, the gods are different aspects of the one reality, Brahman. Just as there are many avatars of Vishnu, there are other gods like Shiva or Kali, but all of them are finite if glorious beings which are aspects of the one supreme Self. If Vishnu or Shiva are said by some to be the supreme God, that is because they are felt by their devotees to be the most adequate images of the nature of the Supreme. And those gods themselves can appear in many different ways – as Krishna does in chapter 11 of the Bhagavadgita.

Christians may find this odd. Yet there are many different images of Jesus, and the rather Anglo-Saxon one that appears in many Western contexts is unlikely to resemble the historical figure of Jesus, whose appearance is never described in the Bible. It is also possible that God may be incarnate on alien worlds, in many different forms. The Indian traditions have much less trouble than Christians have had in thinking of the universe as unimaginably vast in space and time, and in thinking of multiple avatars (incarnations?) of the Lord. In this respect, even though Hindu thought did not have scientific knowledge of the universe and of cosmic evolution, it did have a much less human-centred perspective on the nature of reality, and therefore a wider vision in many ways of the grandeur and power of God.

Christians can say that stories of Krishna are probably not founded on historical fact, while the story of Jesus is founded on events that happened in recorded history. Yet Hindus can reply that the history is not important in itself, but as a sign or manifestation of spiritual truth. Even if Krishna was not a historical person who danced with milkmaids or balanced a mountain on his fingertips, he is a symbol of a loving and joyful spiritual personality which is real and enduring. They may add that some stories about Jesus may also be legendary, and were recorded to convey spiritual truths rather than to be diaries of events. Debates of this sort may not be, as a Buddhist might say, profitable for salvation or enlightenment. It is plausible to think that both Krishna and Jesus can be taken to show that devotion to a personalised image of the Supreme Lord is an authentic way to union with the divine.

I do not suppose that there is any way in which Hinduism, in any of its many forms, will agree entirely with Christianity. But then Christians do not even agree among themselves. Agreement is not the goal of positive and creative interaction between religious traditions. The goal is a widening of understanding that is prepared to learn from other traditions. There are many religious communities where this is happening. The Benedictine monk Bede Griffiths founded an ashram (a monastery) in India, where Christian thought is shaped by Indian sages like Sankara and Ramanuja rather than by ancient Greeks like Plato and Aristotle.[25] There are many other enterprises of the same sort in many parts of the world. These are the creative points of religion. Christian thought is being shaped by global interactions which are focussed on the meeting of different particular traditions, not on facile generalisations about systems which are viewed as alien and inferior, and which exclude any real sharing of life between them. That is why

[25] Bede Griffiths has written many books; one on this theme is *The Marriage of East and West* (London: Collins, 1982).

general condemnations of religion like Barth's are not helpful in try-ing to bring peace and reconciliation to the world – even though that is surely one of Barth's major concerns. Those concerns are shown in some of his later works. But they are not shown in volume I, part 2, of the *Dogmatics*, and that has given rise to unfortunate uses of Barth's theology when some Christians consider the world religions.

East Asian Religions

Although Barth does consider Jodo-Shin-Shu, which is a Japanese form of Buddhism, it is a very unusual form of Buddhism, which manages to include devotion and faith in a form of religion which traditionally has no belief in a personal, supreme God. Barth does not consider the main forms of East Asian religion at all, which include most forms of Buddhism, but they are genuine forms of religion, and so ought to fall under his condemnation of them as self-justifying and having a wilful notion of God. Such condemna-tion seems inappropriate, however, because they are in general not concerned with self-justification or with God at all.

It would be absurd to try to treat of East Asian religions in any depth, but it is important to note how very different they are from the sorts of religion Barth talks about. It may seem much more dif-ficult to find the presence and activity of God in them, but I will sketch some points which may make it seem less difficult.

In China, Taoism, for example, does not have the idea of one per-sonal creator, who has a positive moral purpose for creation. It does have the idea of a spiritual or non-material basis for the universe, but it is not considered to be morally or even ontologically perfect. That is, it is not a sort of sum of all admirable qualities. It is the ineffable Tao, or Way; 'The Tao that can be expressed is not the eternal Tao.'[26] From it all things derive, but they are not generated for the sake of producing goodness. Heaven and earth contain both good and bad, both Yin and

---

[26] *Tao Te Ching*, trans. D. C. Lau (London: Penguin, 1953), 1, 1.

Yang. The Tao itself is 'empty'; it does not seek to dominate things, but is a source of many forms of finite being, of life and death, of good and evil. Nevertheless, nature, with its joy and suffering, is the expression of the Tao, and the Taoist way is one of harmony with nature.

Harmony with the ways of nature is commended, as is an acceptance of pleasurable and unpleasant experiences without joy or resentment, with inner stillness. One chief characteristic of a Taoist life is *wu-wei*, acting without acting, or letting things be themselves, without interfering. However, many forms of Taoism embrace devotion to 'Heavenly Masters' who may be said to express the Tao, and it is often permissible to worship many gods or even one Supreme Lord, Laozi, or revered ancestors, though all these beings are subordinate to the Tao. It is more like a form of life than like a credal faith, but it has temples and rituals, can take many institutional forms, and has been considered part of the single functioning system of the religious life of China, which comprises Taoism, Buddhism, especially Ch'an (or Zen) Buddhism, and Confucianism.

A major Chinese religion, Confucianism, is very different in many ways, being much more concerned with social harmony, the importance of family, and living according to strict moral standards.[27] But it too shows little interest in one creator God, although *tian*, Heaven, is sometimes given a personal form, and life is to be lived in conformity with the 'way of Heaven'.

One might say that, philosophically speaking, these religions are not so much concerned with gods as with the right way of living in accordance with nature (Taoism), or an objective moral order (Confucianism), or a right view of the transience of all things (Buddhism). But devotion to personal Immortals or ancestors as well as local deities are important in practice, and there are many stories of 'revelations', visions, and possessions by exalted spiritual beings. So in Chinese religious traditions one can find anything from silent meditation to fortune-telling and rituals to bring good luck.

---

[27] See the *Analects of Confucius*, available on many websites.

This is a very different religious world from that of Abrahamic religions, which tend to be much more exclusive and doctrine-centred. Apart from all the local cults of gods, ancestors, and Immortals which tend to be combined with the great traditions, the emphasis is on living in harmony with the 'way of Heaven' or with nature, seen as the manifestation of the Tao. Techniques of meditation and ceremonial rituals are taught systematically.

Apart from the monastic orders in Buddhism and Taoism, religion tends to focus on private devotions and visits to various temples. There is no great emphasis on sin or redemption, though there is an awareness of an unnameable spiritual basis for all things, and the cultivation of inner stillness and good-heartedness in personal life. This is just about as different from Christianity as religions can get. Yet overall, East Asian religion cannot be called self-centred, nor can it be accused of arbitrarily inventing fantastic pictures of God. On the contrary, it seeks to conform the individual self to a cosmic or social order, to speak of gods as revealed, appearing in visions to devotees, and to subordinate the gods to an ineffable supreme reality.

If one takes a Christian view that God wills all humans to achieve happiness in loving the divine, one would have to say that this is not the focus of East Asian religions. But one could say that in seeking to follow the 'way of Heaven', or of the Tao, there are disciplines of training which lead to an openness to a transcendent spiritual reality, and a preparedness to live in accordance with what is perceived to be its nature. That may well be enough to be at least a preparation for life with God. It does not seem to be, as Barth's view would suggest, a self-centred and arbitrary opposition to goodness and truth, worthy only of condemnation by a good and loving God.

Religious Diversity and Salvation

As one looks at the variety of religious paths in the world, it seems that there is a general human concern with a spiritual, non-material, basis of existence. Humans can have some awareness of this, but they will describe it in ways which differ largely because of differences in the basic values of their culture.[28] Some will think of a personal, rational, wholly good, supreme being. Others will think that the supreme reality must be more than personal, be the source of evil as well as goodness, and not be limited by the constraints of human rational thought. Some will think that the world is a realm of greed, hatred, and ignorance. Others will think that the world is an expression of creative love. Some will think that the world is destined for destruction, and that escape from it is desirable. Others will think that the world is destined to realise a loving communion, and that it can be transformed by human endeavour.

These differences in basic human attitudes are found within virtually all religions. But various traditions stress some attitudes more than others. Barth's theology emphasises the existence of a personal God of severe judgment, gracious forgiveness, and sovereign and predetermining purpose. He finds this expressed (though admittedly ambiguously) in Protestant Christianity, and to be exclusively revealed in Jesus Christ.

A central question with which this book is concerned is what such a view has to say about the huge diversity of religious and philosophical beliefs in the world. Barth thinks that it will condemn all beliefs, including even the true ones, apparently. But then it will select some, and only the Evangelical Protestant ones, to be both true and efficacious for salvation. I suggest that, whatever one thinks about this, it is not morally or spiritually acceptable to say that one has to be an Evangelical Protestant to be saved. Maybe one does not even have to be a Christian. Perhaps Barth would agree with this, and what happens to the rest of the world is left open. But no plausible mechanism for procuring the salvation of those in all the 'false' religions is made clear.

---

[28] I have given a fuller justification for this claim, and an account of the variety and types of religion, in *The Case for Religion* (London: Oneworld, 2004), especially in part II.

3 | The Revolt against Liberalism

Barth's Relation to German Liberal Theology

When Barth speaks of religion he is not really concerned with considering the whole range of religions throughout the world. His concern is with developments in Christian theology, and in particular developments in German theology, since the Reformation. He is influenced by people like Kant, Schleiermacher, Hegel, Harnack, and Otto. Immanuel Kant (born 1724) was not a theologian, and never attended a Christian church, but his Critiques of Reason were very influential in the growth of German Idealism. Schleiermacher (born 1768) tried to see Christianity as one case of evoking a 'sense of the Infinite' among others. Hegel (born 1770) thought that religion provided picturesque versions of Idealist philosophy. Harnack (born 1851) purged Christian faith of most of its literal historical claims. And Otto (born 1869) found a universal religious sense in the idea of the 'numinous', a sense of mystery, terror, and attraction unique to religion.

Barth, reacting against his own early training in liberal theology and in German Idealism, and shocked by the acceptance, by liberal theologians like Harnack, of German militaristic nationalism, set out to demolish their influence. His case was that Jesus Christ was not just the founder of one religious tradition among others, but a unique and one-time revelation of God. Christianity was not just a largely mythical way of supporting an independently known moral life, as Kant had proposed. It was a revealed truth, which needed no philosophical foundation to justify it.

It is Barth's defence of this case with which this part of the *Church Dogmatics* is concerned. I shall consider his work page by page, and argue in detail that his defence not only fails, but supports an uncharitable and potentially damaging account of Christian faith. It is uncharitable, because it views all religions as displeasing to God, and this means that they are viewed as ultimately misleading. It is damaging, because it holds that only Protestant religion is 'sublimated' by God so that, despite being displeasing to God, it becomes 'the site' of the truth about God and the only medium of divine forgiveness and sanctification. This has the effect of threatening to limit the grace of God to one tiny religious system, and regarding all other spiritual paths as ineffective for salvation.

In his later writings, Barth modified these rigorous views, though he never wrote explicitly and fully about religion again. Especially in *Dogmatics*, volume IV, part 3, para. 69, he speaks about Christ as the light of the world, and stresses that Christ is the only light of the world, and the source of all other lights, which derive from Christ whether people realise it or not. But there are other lights and even other forms of revelation, it seems. After affirming that Christ is the only true light, he says, 'Nor does it follow from our statement ... that all the lights that rise and shine in this outer sphere [outside the Christian faith] are misleading and all the revelations are necessarily untrue.'[1] On the contrary, there are 'other lights which are quite clear and other revelations which are quite real'.

This seems to be a remarkable admission, in view of what Barth has said in *Dogmatics* volume I, part 2, where he regards all religions as displeasing to God and ineffective for salvation. There is indeed a marked change of tone. Yet he continues to regard all religions as displeasing to God, distinguishing between what religions say and the revelation of Jesus Christ. He also regards all religions other than the Christian as ineffective for salvation, since only Christianity is the site of the saving truth of Christ's death and resurrection for us.

---

[1] Barth, *Church Dogmatics*, volume IV, part 3, p. 97.

What in his later work he affirms is that there are nevertheless truths in other religions; they are not totally false. Christians may listen to other faiths; they are not unworthy of attention. Yet, despite what he says, they remain misleading, for they lack the one thing needful for salvation, which is faith in Jesus Christ.

The later Barth thus comes to a more positive view of world religions, a view which he now sees as having been already implicit in his key belief that God in Christ has decisively united human nature to the divine nature, and declared the divine will for the justification and sanctification of humanity as such. If that is true, God cannot have restricted his concern only to Christians, or only to Protestant Reformed Christians at that. God must have a universal concern for the whole world. 'The revelation of man's exaltation to living fellowship with God as this has been achieved in the person of the Son' is 'the revelation of the reconciliation of the world with God'.[2]

However, Barth's often repeated assertion that in Christ God has taken away the sin of the world, and has reconciled the world with God, is more mysterious than it seems. The death of Christ has not literally taken away the sin of the world, for sin remains very obviously present. A more nuanced account is needed. One possibility is to say that Christ's passion and death have removed the natural consequence of sin, which is estrangement from God. As God in Jesus shared in the sufferings and estrangement of humanity, so God showed that God would continue to share in that estrangement as long as it lasted, and would deprive it of its wholly destructive consequences (the 'spiritual death' of separation from God).

Christ's resurrection and raising to union with God does not actually reconcile the world completely to God, since even faithful Christians do not yet know God clearly and love God fully. Rather, God calls humans to repent of sin and trust in God, empowers them gradually to do so, and promises that they will ultimately be wholly reconciled to God in complete obedience and love.

[2] Ibid., p. 116.

When Barth says, as the Bible puts it, that God has reconciled the world to God,[3] it cannot mean that God has done this in the past, so that there is nothing more for humans to do. The meaning is not fully clear, as can be seen from the different theological interpretations of it that have been offered. But it could (and I think it does) mean that God has, by the resurrection of Jesus, shown that the world can and will be fully reconciled to God, and that reconciliation can begin now in this life.

So the reconciliation effected in Jesus is not a one-time and completed past event. It is the historical exemplification of a continuing divine process of reconciliation.

Reconciliation is not a divinely completed process that requires no human response. On the contrary, it may continue only if humans respond to God's invitation by repentance and obedient trust. Reconciliation usually requires action on the part of both parties which seek reconciliation. Even God cannot reconcile humanity if humanity does not seek or accept reconciliation. And that means that the reconciliation of the world could be desired and initiated by God, but it might not include the whole world. It does, however, include all who respond.

Further, if the world has been reconciled to God in Christ, then it must in some sense be replete with the presence and activity of God. 'We cannot possibly think that He cannot speak, and His speech cannot be attested, outside this sphere [this narrower and smaller sphere of the Bible and the Church].'[4]

So Barth can say 'the creaturely world ... has also its own true lights and truths'.[5] It sounds as though Christians should listen for the voice of God in many different forms outside the Christian faith. The Holy Spirit is active in many ways, and if the Spirit speaks, one would think that people can hear and be transformed insofar as they

---

[3] 2 Corinthians 5, 18–20.

[4] Barth, *Church Dogmatics*, volume IV, part 3, p. 117.

[5] Ibid., p. 139.

are open to the power of God, and they can be not just condemned as sinners, but accepted as destined for fellowship with God. They can even be 'esteemed' by God.[6] It sounds as though Barth is holding that many religions and forms of belief can lead to God, though Christianity has some sort of superiority in that it alone has the full truth about God and salvation.

That, however, would undermine almost the whole of the section on religion in the *Dogmatics*, and Barth explicitly says that his later work is 'not in opposition' to that paragraph.[7] There must be some other explanation for this 'change of direction'. There is, and it lies in his claim that, while there are indeed true lights and truths outside faith in Jesus Christ, they are in fact 'secondary forms of the Word of God'.[8] They are true only insofar as they are reflections or reproductions of the Word, or at least do not conflict with it.

It is not the case that there are many revelations of religious truth, and Jesus happens to be the best of them. That is the liberal fallacy, for Barth. Rather, there is one wholly true revelation, and from within the fold of that revelation one can see that there will be many partial intimations of it, and many examples throughout the whole world of human experience of what are in fact the providential actions of the one God revealed uniquely in Jesus.

One can see that many intimations of beauty, wisdom, and love can be found outside the sphere of Christian faith. But one can also see that they are really echoes of the voice and presence of the God of Jesus Christ, and they can be identified correctly only when this is seen. Since these intimations are often given in the context of religions, they must still be displeasing to God insofar as they are entangled with false images of God and self-centred desires, misleading if taken as in themselves showing the true nature of salvation, and ineffective in themselves to lead to salvation.

---

[6] Barth, *The Humanity of God*, p. 51.
[7] Ibid., p. 37.
[8] Barth, *Church Dogmatics*, volume IV, part 3, p. 113.

That seems to be where Barth ends his discussion of religion. Is it an uncharitable and damaging account? He has done much in his later work to counter the charge that it is. It is, however, important that he never suggests that non-Christian religions are sublimated so as to become real vehicles of salvation. They do contain intimations of divine presence and activity, but they remain mired in the unfaithfulness of religion. They fail to recognise that humans are saved only by the death and resurrection of Jesus Christ, and Christianity alone is the site, the decisive revelation, of God's saving action.

But I also think that one sees here the beginnings of a rather different view that Barth never explicitly affirms, but that could be seen as an expansion of his later and uncompleted thought. That is, that though Christianity contains the fully authentic path to freedom from sin and fellowship with God, there are elements of true goodness in human nature and even in human spirituality and religion. There are spiritual truths to be found outside the Christian faith, and human persons may begin effectively to turn to the ultimate reality which is God in many different ways. Such a view is not as far from Christian liberalism as Barth thought when he wrote *Church Dogmatics*, volume I, part 2.

Immanuel Kant

Immanuel Kant is one of the most famous philosophers of the European Enlightenment. He even defined the Enlightenment as 'Man's release from his ... inability to make use of his understanding'.[9] When he applied his understanding to the traditional proofs of God, he found them all wanting. Barth would have approved of that. Nevertheless, Kant believed in God, and was what he called

[9] *What Is Enlightenment?* [1784], trans. Lewis White Beck, in Immanuel Kant, *On History* (Indianapolis: Bobbs-Merrill, 1963), p. 3.

a 'critical Idealist'.[10] He believed that reality in-itself was mind-like (noumenal), and that the physical universe was an appearance of that unknowable reality. He even believed in the possibility of immortal life, and that immortal life could be, and could only be, obtained by some unknown and incomprehensible moral help from God.[11] When he wrote about Christianity, however, he regarded it as an almost totally mythical or symbolic account to support obedience to the moral law, and he virtually denied the possibility of any experience of God. Philosophical Idealism after Kant often did not use the word 'God'. Hegel, for instance, talked of *Geist*, or Absolute Spirit. Barth definitely did not approve of that, and denied that philosophy had any place in theology, or needed to be used to provide a foundation for Christian faith. That was partly, no doubt, why he accused Enlightenment, or liberal, thinking about religion as having an arbitrarily devised idea of God, and a wilful concern with self-justification.

In thinking this, Barth is guilty of a totally unjust understanding of Kant. Kant did not have an 'arbitrarily devised image of God'. On the contrary, his concept of God is, for better or worse, basically a continuation of the 'perfect being' theology which is the standard Christian theological belief that goes back to antiquity.[12] God is a postulate of reason, an ideal of perfection whose existence, according to Kant, cannot be proved by reason, but who must be posited as a condition of making sense of the absolute moral obligation to pursue happiness in accordance with virtue (or excellence) for all. His God is omnipotent, omniscient, and perfectly good, just like the God Barth worshipped.

[10] 'I desire this idealism of mine to be called critical', Immanuel Kant, *Prolegomena*, trans. John Mahaffy and John Bernard (London: Macmillan, 1889), 'How Is Pure Mathematics Possible?', Remark 3, p. 48.
[11] Immanuel Kant, *Religion within the Boundaries of Mere Reason*, trans. Allen Wood (Cambridge: Cambridge University Press, 2018), pp. 76–84.
[12] See Immanuel Kant, *Critique of Pure Reason*, trans. Norman Kemp Smith (London: Macmillan, 1952), Transcendental Dialectic, section 2, 'The Transcendental Ideal'.

It is also the height of irony to accuse Kant of 'wilful' concern with justifying and sanctifying himself, when Kant is the apostle of absolute and categorical moral demands (derived from the Categorical Imperative), which are rooted in transcendent reality. For Kant, concern with personal fulfilment, though it properly exists, must be completely and unequivocally subordinated to unquestioning obedience to the moral law, which has an objective existence and a complete authority over human lives. This is not a self-serving view. Kant's exposition of religion is entitled *Religion within the Boundaries of Mere Reason*, so it does not have much truck with revelation. But in it, Kant rather shamefacedly admits an appeal to some incomprehensible help from God, and holds that reason has its limits which in the end need to be complemented by faith.[13] German Idealism may not always have been friendly to Christian belief, as Barth understood it, but it does not deserve the contempt which Barth pours upon it.

Friedrich Schleiermacher

A more important influence on Barth was Friedrich Schleiermacher, for whom Barth professes a certain admiration. Schleiermacher's writings were in the first instance for the cultured despisers of religious belief, and were intended to show that Christianity was not just about a wholly miraculous breaking of the laws of nature by God. It was not either a complicated metaphysical system or an ethical teaching. It was an integral part of the intellectual and cultural life of humanity, and was concerned with the fulfilment of the deepest feelings (*Gefühle*) and intuitions (*Anschauungen*) of human life. He wrote in a culture where criticism of the Bible on both historical and moral grounds had become widespread, and where the natural

---

[13] Ibid., preface to 2nd ed., p. 22: 'I have therefore found it necessary to deny knowledge, in order to make room for faith.'

sciences had virtually demolished belief in angels and demons who pushed the planets around or caused diseases. The application of critical historical methodology to the Bible had resulted in scepticism about the historical accuracy of the Gospels. The widespread rejection by the natural sciences of any purpose in nature, and the discovery of apparently absolute but blind laws of nature had led to the rejection of any appeal to a providential God.

Schleiermacher's proposal was that religion was not about believing in miraculous events which were not very well evidenced, produced by a God who interfered in nature on rare occasions. It was about cultivating a sense and taste for the Infinite, or what he later called a sense of absolute dependence.

'All the divine attributes ... are only meant to explain the feeling of absolute dependence.'[14] This led him to be one of the first theologians to speak about religion as virtually universal to human societies. He then argued that Christianity was 'more sublime, more worthy of adult humanity' than other religions.[15]

Barth objected to both the very vague notion of God that this seemed to provide, and to the idea that Christianity was only one religion among others. He saw that the superiority of Christianity was very doubtful on this view, and that it would not be long before Christianity was seen as just one option among others in the religious world – a possibility that was realised in the work of Troeltsch.[16] So Barth insisted that Jesus was the one real revelation of a personal and redeeming God, not just an allegedly superior form of piety or religiosity. He was also very suspicious of the notion of 'piety', as it seemed to reduce religion to a form of subjective feeling, and to replace knowledge of truth with intensity of feeling.

[14] Friedrich Schleiermacher, *The Christian Faith*, trans. H. R. Mackintosh and J. S. Stewart (Edinburgh: T. and T. Clark, 1989), p. 225.

[15] Friedrich Schleiermacher, *On Religion*, trans. Richard Crouter (Cambridge: Cambridge University Press, 1988) p. 213.

[16] See my *Religion in the Modern World* (Cambridge: Cambridge University Press, 2019), chapter 22, for my comments on Troeltsch.

This is not fair to Schleiermacher, as by 'feeling' he meant a cognitive grasp of some reality, not just an inner feeling. This cognition is associated with intense feelings of awe and dependence. But these feelings have an objective reference, even if the object is rather vague – Schleiermacher characterised it as 'the Infinite', or later on as the absolutely independent. Perhaps what Schleiermacher did not take account of is that the objects of religious feeling are quite different in many religions. A feeling that one is encountering a personal creator, as in Christianity, is different from a feeling that one is apprehending the insubstantiality of being, as in Buddhism. To speak of something like 'a sense of transcendence' may be a useful general term which signifies that one apprehends something that is not a material object or a collection of such objects. But it needs to be further specified, and such specification cannot rely entirely on the subjective character of the feeling. No inspection of human psychological states can assure one that one apprehends an omnipotent creator, or that one apprehends an impersonal supreme consciousness. Religions, and religious feelings, may be much more varied than Schleiermacher thought – his own notions of 'the Infinite' and of the 'absolutely independent' even seem to be rather different from each other.

Although Barth admired Schleiermacher, he nevertheless held that religion was not just a matter of feeling. It was grounded firmly in objective facts. But where accounts of those objective facts differed from the Christian revelation, they were false.

However, it seems that many claims of non-Christians do not differ from some Christian claims, so there may be much truth in other religions. And it also seems that many things some Christians have claimed are false – Barth, for instance, thought the liberal theologians had many false beliefs. One needs to be careful to discover which Christian accounts are true, and it may seem very odd and even rather arrogant if one sect of Christians is said to have the only completely true account. It is also no longer so different from liberal Christianity, if truth is granted to other faiths, but Christianity is said to have a better grasp of truth. That seems just another way of saying, as Schleiermacher did, that Christianity is a more sublime and complete form of religious truth.

Adolf von Harnack

A theologian to whom Barth came to be in almost total opposition was Adolf Harnack, under whom Barth had studied at the University of Berlin. He was perhaps the best-known German theologian of his day, and he argued that Biblical scholarship had shown the New Testament to be a work that presented a picture of Jesus very different from that of the historical figure. What Jesus was really like had to be built up by careful research into the legendary elements of the Gospels and into the religious life of ancient Israel. Harnack's conclusion was that Jesus was a great spiritual teacher and probably a faith healer, but that it was unrealistic to think of him as an incarnation of God who died for the sins of the world. He wrote that in 'God the Father, Providence, the position of men as God's children, the infinite value of the human soul – the whole Gospel is expressed'.[17] There was a God who cared for creation, there was a purpose in creation, which was that humans should attain happiness and fulfilment. Humans were of infinite value, and they were 'children of God', realising the rule of God in their lives. This teaching, he thought, was the core of religion, and nothing more was needed – no abstruse arguments about the Trinity, no theories of atonement through the sacrifice of blood, and no miraculous events proving that Jesus was a god-man. There was a supreme morality of love, revealed by Jesus, aided by the inner working of God's Spirit, and supported by the promise of future fulfilment. That was enough, and it was what Jesus had taught as

---

[17] Adolf Harnack, *What Is Christianity?*, trans. Thomas Bailey Saunders (Minneapolis: Fortress Press, 1984), Lecture 4, p. 87.

the 'coming of the Kingdom', the rule of God in the hearts of men and women.

When Harnack signed 'The Manifesto of the Ninety-Three' in 1914, in which ninety-three German intellectuals supported Germany's military actions in the First World War, Barth felt that there was something wrong with a theology which could justify war in this way. He came to think that the basic mistake was to ally Christian belief with the culture and politics of nation states. Jesus Christ, he wrote, undermined any form of subordination of faith to political leaders or cultural norms. The Gospel was deeply countercultural, and Barth sent to Hitler his protest that allegiance to the Lordship of Christ forbade any allegiance to the supremacy of human dictators.

Harnack's signing of that document is indeed worrying, but there is really little in his theology that would justify it. A theology of the rule of the Spirit of Love in human hearts hardly suggests a participation in a tragic and destructive war in which millions will be killed.

But it seems that a wholly commendable belief in the love of God given to all humans co-existed in Harnack with a belief that Germany was justified in promoting violent warfare. I would not think it fair to call this total corruption. It was a call for goodness that was perverted by mistaken political beliefs. Such a thing had also been seen in Luther's violent reaction to the Peasants' Revolt, so it is not unique to liberal theologians.

The evidence of history suggests that our best endeavours for goodness and justice are liable to corruption, but not that these endeavours themselves are corrupt. Logic suggests that where there is corruption, there is something intrinsically good that is being corrupted. For these reasons, I do not think it is a reasonable reaction to liberal theology to condemn such religious beliefs as faithless, or to think of liberal faith as responsible in some way for a capitulation to political evil.

It is true that many German Christians supported the Nazi regime of Hitler, and used Christianity as a support for a repressive political ideology. Barth's opposition to such Christians, expressed in the Barmen Declaration, which he mostly wrote, is well known and rightly applauded. Many German liberal theologians supported Hitler. But I think that their mistake was not that they had abandoned traditional Christianity, but that they were not liberal enough. True liberalism is opposed to tyranny and persecution of minorities or of the socially disadvantaged. It is strange that even liberals like Kant, whose philosophy advocated the moral equality and dignity of all human beings, failed to see that his ethical rules applied to women as well as men. Enlightenment morality opposes all unjustified social hierarchies and inequalities, and that should have been perceived.

Unfortunately, the very sense that a superior morality had here been adopted led to a belief that this culture was itself superior to others which were still primitive by comparison. So the theoretical belief in the dignity of all was in practice still associated with a sense of cultural and social inequality. The antidote to this should have been to see that equality and democracy were implications of liberalism, and that they were in fact implicit in the Christian Gospel too. Precisely because of that, the Gospel needed to be freed from the shackles of authoritarian traces of thought from which even the apostles were not yet free.[18] Christianity needed to be more, not less, liberal.

Of course, there are religions which are immoral, which are self-deceiving, and which aim to get power and foment hatred. But there are also religions which just make honest mistakes. Barth is rightly honoured for his stand against the Nazi Party in Germany. But was he right in claiming that 'one is defenceless against the "German Christians", unless one has already lodged a well-founded protest' against liberalism in religion (87)? The subordination of Christian teaching to alien cultural norms is not a distinctive feature

---

[18] Romans 13, 1: 'Let every person be subject to the governing authorities, for there is no authority except from God.'

of liberal theology. It has in fact been more typical of conservative Christian views, ever since Christianity became the official faith of the despotic Roman Empire. Over the centuries, many Christians since the time of Constantine have supported violent and repressive regimes. In this century, the patriarch of the Russian Orthodox Church has publicly supported the destruction of innocent adults and children in Ukraine by a ruthless Russian dictator. It is often orthodox Christians, not the liberals, who have undermined their faith by supporting violent oppression of others.

Liberals, like conservatives, often fail to see the contradiction between Jesus' teaching of non-violent resistance[19] and their own conduct. That can give rise to the feeling that religion is intrinsically faithless and dangerous. It often is. But in most forms of religion it is not the powerful leaders of churches who show what faith really requires. It is the unknown heroes, the martyrs of faith, who in humble obedience to the teaching of Jesus, turn the other cheek, love their enemies, and die.

Nor does liberal theology, as such, lead to making Jesus a peripheral add-on to an independent definition of religion – another of Barth's reasons for opposing German Christian liberalism. Jesus can still be seen as the Incarnation of the Eternal Word, who is the saviour of the whole world. A liberal Christian faith is one that is committed to the search for truth, to the avoidance of stereotyping and unduly negative perceptions of competing faiths, and to ways of positively interacting with people of differing opinions insofar as that is possible, so as to avoid misunderstanding, hatred, violence, and bloodshed.

The Search for Truth

Barth's reactions to German liberal theology, while understandable in their context, seem questionable. But in an examination of religion as such, it needs to be noted that Barth is restricting what he

---

[19] Matthew 5, 43: 'Love your enemies.'

calls 'religion' (that which is to be sublimated) to largely German, either Protestant or liberal, forms of theistic belief. That is a severely restricted view of what religion is.

I would not myself think it wise to give a definition of 'religion' which could cover every actual and possible case. But we can see, and in fact Barth sees, that many religions posit a non-material, more powerful and valuable, reality to which humans can relate. When groups are organised to encourage that interest, they may fairly be called religions. There are, of course, many imaginative constructions in religion. There are many differences in beliefs about an ultimate reality, and they cannot all be correct. But it is simply mistaken to condemn all efforts to find the truth in such matters as wilful and arbitrary. The human concern to seek truth and understanding is an honourable one.

Anyone who said that seeking truth about the universe in physics just gives rise to wilful and arbitrary concepts, and is concerned just to increase human self-importance and pride, would rightly be considered misanthropic, a hater of humanity, and pathologically gloomy. Why should the search for truth in religion be different? By his definition of religion Barth threatens almost to be a misanthropic hater of humanity. Again, in his later work, Barth tries to counter this charge, by stressing that man is also redeemed by God, and therefore should be valued as such.[20] But in his condemnation of all human searches for the truth about God, Barth is in danger of treating all humans who think of religion as a human search for truth as wholly evil and abominated by God.

In contrast, it has always seemed to me a Christian axiom that to seek truth and goodness for its own sake, however personally pleasant or unpleasant, is a great human good.[21] Of course humans start

[20] 'Through His own election He willed man to be His creature, His partner, and His Son': 'The Gift of Freedom', in Barth, *The Humanity of God*, p. 79.

[21] See Paul's letter to the Romans 2, 7: 'To those who by persistence in doing good seek glory, honour, and immortality, he [God] will give eternal life.'

with ignorance about the nature of ultimate reality, and the truth is not just 'given' to them in some magical way. It has to be found by trial and error, and it involves argument and critical engagement with others. We should honour those who are prepared even to risk their lives in the search for truth – and this would include many of those who were called 'heretics' in their day. There will be many mistakes and imperfections in the search for truth, in religion as in most human activities, but that search should not be considered sinful. On the contrary, it should be praised and encouraged, in the hope that it will enable human understanding to grow. It would be not only stupid but morally questionable to suggest that everyone who sincerely seeks for religious truth, and critically examines all such claims to truth, is wilful and arbitrary.

True Religion

Despite his gloomy view of religion (it surely is a gloomy view which sees religion as self-centred and wilful), Barth writes, 'the church is the site of the true religion' (37). I suggest that there is a huge category mistake in even talking about a true religion. Propositions can be true or false; they can state the facts accurately or not. But religion cannot be true or false, any more than music or art can. Truth, while it is very important, may only be one element to take into account when thinking about religion. It is misleading to say that there is only one wholly true religion, instead of considering various truth-claims within religions that may overlap, interact, and change over time.

Ninian Smart proposed a seven-dimensional analysis of religion which stressed that it is not just propositional truths that constitute a religion.[22] Other features, like ethical rules, ritual practices, social

---

[22] Ninian Smart, *The World's Religions* (Cambridge: Cambridge University Press, 1989), introduction, and *Secular Education and the Logic of Religion* (London: Faber, 1968).

structures, personal experiences, treasured myths, and aesthetic values may for many believers constitute more important features of religion.

For many Christians, for example, propositional truths or doctrines are not of great importance. They would not be interested in theological debates about the Trinity or the Atonement, and they might have very individual interpretations of the things they hear in church. They can hear that God loves them, that there is always hope even in times of difficulty, and that they can be devoted to Jesus, without digesting and agreeing with the contents of a two-volume catechism.

Some Christians would think the heart of Christianity lies in its moral teaching, in the practice of love and kindness, and would take many stories in the New Testament as parables to help people to live in a more loving way. It used to be very common in England for people to say 'I am a Christian' when they did not ever go to church or recite a creed.

Others may find ritual practices, like the celebration of Mass, to be important parts of their lives. They might not want to have elaborate explanations of what is going on, but somehow the activities of offering, confessing, praying, and receiving can be behavioural expressions and shapers of a form of life, circling around a spiritual dimension to their lives, while the actual words used are employed for their emotive effect rather than their literal meaning.

There are many for whom the communal life of a church, with its friendships and little hierarchies and responsibilities, is of the first importance. Some, but by no means all, will have profound spiritual experiences, even visions or inspirations, which they find corroborated by a community which takes such things seriously, and does not merely mock them. Or they may find the practice of meditation or contemplation of great personal value, while not being too troubled about whatever beliefs are said by some to underlie such techniques. And some will find the beauty of music, architecture, art, and liturgy, to be conveyers of a sense of transcendence and peace.

I have spoken only of Christians, but this variety of responses would generally hold for believers in many religions. What it shows is that religious belief is not only a matter of accepting some propositional beliefs. Indeed, for many that is not of great significance, even though believers with a very rationalistic cast of mind (like me, perhaps) may try to persuade others that it is. On the whole, Western Christian churches have tended to prioritise propositional beliefs, and have constructed creeds to say what these beliefs are. Yet even creeds are recited in worship, and are then more like hymns or recitations of a sacred story than like formal statements of what one has to believe. After all, few people who sing hymns loudly and enthusiastically have to believe everything they sing.

Many religions do not have creeds, and have a much more relaxed attitude to what their adherents think. In many East Asian countries people can attend Buddhist, Taoist, or Confucian temples when they feel like it. Different institutions do have different doctrines, of course, but that is not always what divides them, and it is their rituals and social customs which mostly distinguish them. Apart from professional priests, devotees are left to participate in different 'religions' according to taste. A serious study of religions is liable to show that propositional beliefs are much less important to the phenomenon of religion than intellectual writers tend to think. Even the propositional beliefs may be interpreted in symbolic, rather than straightforward, ways.

Still, there obviously are propositions in religion, and these may be true or false. There may be particular beliefs of some church that are true; there may be some beliefs of that church that are false; and there may be some about which many members remain undecided. But to say that a whole church or a whole religion is true is just like saying that England is true, or that the Houses of Parliament are true. It just does not make sense. It may be used in a poetic or metaphorical sense, but it is still a grammatical mistake. Religions are ways of life, not catalogues of beliefs.

To the extent that there are truth-claiming propositions in religion, we just have to decide which of them we accept. We do what Barth actually does in the *Church Dogmatics*, and look at the various arguments in (and outside) our church (if we have one) over the years. We assess the criticisms made and the reasons given, to take one example, for the belief that God will redeem everyone. We may find that the Bible has no clear answer to this question, yet we may still claim that one interpretation seems nearer to the general drift of Biblical teaching as we read it. How do we know that interpretation is the best one? We just have to decide – or, if we take someone else's word (Calvin's or Luther's or Barth's), we just have to decide which of them seems likely to be correct. There is no avoiding this decision, though of course this feels to the believer more like a 'calling' or dawning of an insight than like a personal choosing among options. But it is better that the decision should be made after taking all the reasons and criticisms that we can into account.

Is this process necessarily wilful or arbitrary? It may be. But it need not be, and often it is not. There is no such thing as 'Reason', which delivers information to us without any prejudice or personal feeling. There is just reasoning, partly critical and partly creative, about problems that come to us in the course of thinking about ultimate reality.

Yet it is not true that all attempts by humans to discover truth in religion are self-interested or arbitrary. It is positively good to seek greater understanding and truth in any area of alleged knowledge, including in religion, by reflection and research. In the end, we just have to decide for ourselves, not the nonsensical question of whether some religion is true, but a whole set of questions about whether some particular beliefs (for instance, that all will be saved by God) are true or not.

4 | The Nature of Revelation

Barth's Idea of Revelation

Having considered the ideas of 'sublimation' and 'religion' in Barth's general heading to his long paragraph on religion in *Church Dogmatics*, volume 1, part 2, I will now explore his idea of 'revelation'.

Revelation seems to assume that there is a God, and that God communicates some information to humans that they would otherwise not have. If you believe in God, it seems reasonable to think that God might communicate to humans something about the divine nature and purpose. How will God do this? There must be one or more individuals to whom a revelation is given. These individuals may receive words from a divine source (as the Prophet Mohammed claims to have done). Or they may have a vision of God, as Arjuna did in one Indian tradition. Or they may have their writing directed in a more general way, protected from error and giving new insights into the divine, as many believe is the case with the writers of the New Testament, or even with the pronouncements of the pope *ex cathedra*.

The word 'revelation' is not used in every religion, but there are cognate terms to refer to the authoritative sources of the religion.

For instance, in Confucianism the writings of Confucius, based on his own insights into the correct way of living, rather than on relation to any god, have authority. There is a belief in the right way of living, in accordance with the 'way of Heaven', but little sense of any objective power making for righteousness. It could be seen as a form of transcendental humanism, but it usually claims to be based on privileged insight into the right way of living in relation to a spiritual dimension of reality.

In Buddhism, the experience of liberation from the wheel of suffering gives the teachings of the Buddha and of other enlightened beings authority. Written scriptures, for some sects the Lotus Sutra, contain a correct view of ultimate reality, and bodhisatvas may help to achieve liberation.

In various forms of Hinduism, the Vedas, dictated by the gods, and the teachings of those who are taken to have achieved consciousness of being one with Brahman, have authority. There are many gods who may help to achieve that state, though for most Hindus all the gods are aspects of one, all-including Absolute Real (Brahman).

In Judaism, the law given by God to set apart the Jewish people, the 'inspired' written history of Israel, and the words of the prophets have authority. There are many founding experiences of personal encounter with God, who is said to judge but also to heal and care for his people.

And in Christianity, Jesus is taken to be the human image of God and the mediator of God's Spirit to humanity. His experience of unity with God, his teachings, and his death and resurrection are recorded in an authoritative Scripture, and his Spirit is felt within communities of his disciples.

In all these traditions, written records of teachings are important, and these in turn are based on alleged privileged access to a spiritual reality, whether that access comes by human insight, devotion to a god, or an experience of acquaintance or union with that reality.

It is not appropriate or helpful to say, as Barth does, that all these forms of religious life are ways of self-justification or of arbitrarily devised images of God. On the contrary, they are ways of trying to discover appropriate ways of thinking, feeling, and living in relation to what are felt to be spiritual dimensions of this puzzling universe.

There are very different ways of thinking of such transcendent dimensions – as objective moral laws, as a state liberated from selfish attachments, as union with a Universal Self, as obedience to a personal creator, or as participation in divine love.[1]

Change and Development in Religion

These ways are not unchanging blocks of beliefs which all exclude and oppose one another. They overlap and interact, they change over time, and they generally agree that human language is inadequate to provide exact and complete descriptions of spiritual reality. For instance, the Buddhist teaching that there is no personal creator God was a major influence on the Advaita Vedanta school of Hindu thought, which taught that there is an ultimate reality which is beyond all personal properties.[2] Religious traditions influence one another, both by reaction and in more positive ways.

It sounds as if Barth would deny this, making one minority Christian tradition 'true', while all others are false. Yet he would not have written as he did if he had not been reacting against his own earlier 'liberal' theology, and if he had not been influenced by German Idealism and the Hegelian stress on dialectical thought. His view, like others, is influenced by previous theological and philosophical thought. The Christian view he himself defends includes a set of beliefs about God and salvation which can be set alongside others which are influenced by different cultural histories and contexts.

Barth states that God's revelation is to be found 'in the outpouring of the Spirit', and the judging but reconciling presence of God (141). This is a recognisably religious view, which is founded on the

---

[1] I have given a fuller account of different kinds of revelation in *Religion and Revelation* (Oxford: Oxford University Press, 1994).
[2] See Friedhelm Hardy, 'The Classical Religions of India', in *The Religions of Asia*, ed. Friedhelm Hardy (London: Routledge, 1990), p. 111.

belief that Jesus had unique access to the mind of God, and was filled with the divine Spirit, which he was able to pass on to others. His crucifixion was taken to express the judgment of God on human sin, and his resurrection was believed to express the possibility of eternal life in God. This is the original revelation of Christian faith, and it occurred in and through the person of Jesus.

That is partly a historical statement about what happened in the past, and it is the New Testament which records these things. The believer must therefore trust these records as accurate, at least in their major claims, and must intend to interpret their meaning faithfully.

Then, if religious faith is to be more than a record of what happened in history, there must be, no doubt to various degrees, present personal experiences of the Spirit, and of the judging and reconciling presence of God, which confirm that one is not just talking about some past event. And there will need to be some explanation of what is meant by such terms as God, Spirit, judgment, sanctification, and grace, which may be unfamiliar in the non-Christian world.

This is a very complex process, involving elements of personal experience, the interpretation of Scripture, and the formation and explanation of various propositional beliefs. They are all elements of revelation, and show that the idea of revelation is complex and many-stranded. In the history of Christianity, many decisions about these elements of revelation have been made. They were often, or even usually, disputed, and they have changed considerably over the years. It was not, especially not in Christianity, just a matter of God clearly saying something, which was then written down verbatim.

At the very beginning there were arguments, recorded in the New Testament, about whether or how far the Torah should be kept by followers of Jesus.[3] Later there were arguments about the relation of

---

[3] See Acts 15, which records this dispute at the Council of Jerusalem.

BARTH'S IDEA OF REVELATION

divine predestination and human freedom, about whether humans were born guilty of original sin, and about whether all or only some humans would have eternal life. There was no original revelation which decided these arguments, and some of them have never been conclusively decided. But decisions were made, and churches divided into various camps. Barth belonged to one version of Protestantism, but is it plausible to claim that this alone preserves in complete purity 'God's revelation'?

It rather seems to be one Christian view among many, which suggests that absolute certainty cannot be found in any view, and that we just have to decide among various alternatives what seems right to us. In other words, human reasoning and decision-making are an important part of deciding just what God's revelation is.

Revelation and Certainty

What Barth seems to think is that God chooses some people (from Abraham onwards), and elects them to know the truth, without any prior process of speculation and searching. The problem is that many people throughout the world feel that the truth has been revealed to them, but they differ enormously about what these things are. Believing that one has had the truth revealed to one, and that one is absolutely certain of it, is no guarantee that it is really the case.

Barth accuses people (like Muslims, for example), who claim to have had non-Christian revelations, presumably in all their many different forms, of wilfully making up ideas of God and selfishly attempting to justify themselves before God and attain positive relationships with God. How can Barth know that Christian revelations escape these charges? How can he be sure that all human attempts to understand God are wilful? Or when attempts to know and love God are selfish? How can he judge humanity so severely? Can people not sincerely ask whether there is purpose in human lives, and whether there is intelligence and value in the universe?

Can they not really be thankful for life, and seek the best they know, simply out of the love of truth, beauty, and goodness?

After all, God could have made things easier. God could have sent down a list of all the laws of science, and explained the existence of evil, and guaranteed his word with a few unquestionably miraculous acts. God could have prevented any competing claims to revelation (like Islam) from existing and flourishing. But God did not do this. In the Christian case, the evidence for the resurrection of Jesus is rather poor, is testified by only a few people, and recorded in texts which are not wholly consistent – for instance, was the stone of Jesus' tomb already rolled away when a group of women got there,[4] or did they see an angel roll it away?[5] It does not look, in any actual case, as if the revelation of God was clear to and undeniable by all intelligent persons.

I mean by this that belief in the resurrection cannot be proved by a dispassionate review of the evidence – which it could have been, if Jesus had appeared in his risen form before Pilate, the high priest, and to the general public in the city squares, or, even better, if he regularly appeared today in meetings of the United Nations. He appeared a long time ago and far away, only for short periods of time, and only to his disciples. Even though these appearances were spectacular, they were not overwhelmingly obvious to all people.[6]

There are no doubt good reasons why this is so, and it certainly says something about the nature of revelation. Revelation is given to few, it is never beyond dispute and so is not absolutely certain, and it requires a predisposition to be transformed, or to be open to manifestations of a transcendent reality, interpreted in a specific, though changing, way in a particular culture. Whether it is a matter of hearing and repeating or writing down words, or of experiencing a vivid sense of a divine presence, or of having a vision of such a

---

[4] Luke 24, 2.

[5] Matthew 28, 2.

[6] 'When they saw him, they worshipped him, but some doubted', Matthew 28, 17.

presence, these things come to those who are prepared for them, even if, like St Paul, they get something different from what they expected.

Then, when the revelation is communicated to others, it will be interpreted and elaborated in various ways, as those who accept the revelation try to work out its meaning for their own lives.

This means that learning, reasoning, and deciding, all of them exercising human capacities, are essential to religion. Revelation is not just given to passive observers, who have no decisions to make, and who have no responsibility for what they believe. The exercise of reason is not just a wilful and arbitrary activity; it is deeply involved in the understanding and reception of any alleged revelation.

Of course a theist would not want this process to be a purely human activity. A theist would want God to play some active part. Even a Buddhist or Taoist would appeal to some authoritative source of beliefs relayed by a person who was believed to have greater insight into religious questions, and perhaps some experience of suprahuman, spiritual realities, to a greater extent than most of us do. Revelation or revelatory authority has an important place in most religions.

It is doubtful whether any revelatory experience could be described in the way that it is without quite a considerable history of thought preceding it. For instance, St Paul had to believe in God and know about claims that Jesus had risen before he could describe his experience on the Damascus road as an encounter with the risen Jesus.

Behind the descriptions of encounter with a judging and forgiving God lies a whole history of developing ideas of God in Hebrew thought – ideas of a Spirit of God working in the world and inspiring the prophets, experiences of ritual practices for making atonement for sin, and the formation of hopes for a community of peace and justice ruled by God, the kingdom of God. This long history prepared the way for the sort of beliefs in God's judgment and grace of which Barth and many Christians speak. Barth is of course aware of this. He explicitly says that God's revelation comes 'in the world of human religion'. It is not just a matter of solitary experience, disconnected from all rational thinking about God. Even though Barth characterises religion as a set of 'attempts by man', nevertheless these attempts set the scene for Christian beliefs about sin and redemption.

The Case of Judaism

The doctrinal preparation for the experience of Jesus himself was after all in the Hebrew Bible, the Old Testament. This has become part of Christian revelation. It records a covenant made between God and the Jewish people that was to be fulfilled, Christians believe, in Jesus. So for Barth it is part of divine revelation, not just a product of human religious imagination. The revelation consists in the inspiration of the prophets, the miraculous history of the Exodus from Egypt, the Torah given to Moses, both in writing and orally, and the inspired writings such as the Psalms and Proverbs.

However, it must be admitted that the Jewish religion is different from the Christian religion, and the Jewish understanding of the Hebrew Bible is very different from the Christian one. Christians see God's covenant with Israel as sublimated (I think that word in this case would be wholly appropriate) by God's covenant with all of humanity in Jesus the Messiah. Much of the Torah is repudiated,[7] and the Messiah comes to be interpreted in a way that is much more important than in Judaism, where it is often a rather peripheral belief, and differs markedly from Jewish expectations that the Messiah would bring peace and fulfilment to Israel.

The character of revelation is quite different – in Christianity, there is no written Hebrew law dictated by God, whose every

---

[7] Galatians 5, 2: 'I, Paul, am telling you that if you let yourselves be circumcised, Christ will be of no benefit to you.' And circumcision was a major part of the Torah.

injunction must be obeyed, and in Judaism there is no prophet who is thought to be divine.

This means that there may be experiences of a judging and merciful personal Lord recorded in the Hebrew Bible. But there is no spectacular outpouring of a fully divine Holy Spirit, no saving death and resurrection of a divine saviour, and little thought of an eternal life of sharing in the divine nature. In that case, the revelation of God in the Old Testament must be thought of by Barth as preparatory or incomplete, and in need of sublimation into a more universal and inward covenant of pure grace.

The Hebrew religion was not, as Barth describes religion, just the human pursuit of self-justification in relation to an arbitrarily devised image of God. It was also the vehicle of a revelation of the judging and merciful presence of the true God, even if it was partial and incomplete.

The sublimation of this religion, from a Christian, but obviously not from a Jewish, point of view, was the creation of a new religion, centred on a divine prophet who was crucified and raised from death to sit at the right hand of God.

If this is true, there is at least one religion other than the Christian which was a vehicle of what Barth describes as 'the revelation of God', even if the understanding of that revelation is partial or incomplete.

This is a matter of some consequence for Barth's view that there is only one 'true religion', and that this religion must be centred on Jesus Christ.

Incomplete Revelation

For Barth, religion is sublimated when it is cancelled and yet fulfilled. This makes sense if the Jewish religion is sublimated, cancelled, and yet fulfilled by the revelation of Jesus Christ. The fact that the Old Testament has become part of Christian revelation means that it is part of the revelation of God. Already, before Jesus, it conveyed the Spirit of God poured out through the prophets, and made a judging and reconciling God present in the world of religion. That, for Barth, would mean that the Jewish religion was 'sublimated', in the rather different sense, the sense that is of most importance for Barth, of being cancelled as a humanly constructed religion, and yet fulfilled by being also God's revelation.

Yet Judaism explicitly rejects Jesus as the Messiah, and thus, according to Barth, it will stand condemned of sinful error (87). In the past it was sublimated, in the sense of being a vehicle of God's revelation. But since Jesus came it has lost its sublimation, and become faithless. The tragic history of Christian anti-Semitism looms on the horizon, however foreign that is to Barth's own personal attitudes. Nevertheless, there was one religion other than Christianity which was sublimated by the revelation of God, and thus in Barth's terms 'true', even though it was incomplete.

It seems absurd to say that Judaism lost its belief in the true God – just the same belief that it had long before Jesus was born, and in the same God that Jesus said humans must love – merely because it could not accept that Jesus was the Messiah, the liberator of Israel. It remained true to the revelation it had received, and regarded the belief that Jesus was one with God as heresy. This was an honest belief which seems entirely explicable as such, and not a case of faithless God-rejection. For Barth to see it as faithless is a calumny on God-fearing Jews, and an unwarranted assumption that his religious beliefs alone are those of genuine faith, whereas those who differ from him are lost and faithless.

Once we have the idea of a true, God-inspired if incomplete religious faith, which is not Christianity, a more charitable approach to non-Christian religions opens up. We might expect that a God of boundless mercy would be present and active, if only in an incomplete way, in many religions. Could a universally loving God not appear in judgment and mercy in many forms of religion, each with their own form of personal encounter? Even in non-theistic

Buddhism, would not some sublimation of the preparatory history of religion be possible – for instance, in a sense and feeling of the wisdom and compassion of the Buddha, who in his Enlightenment had passed beyond human form; in a sense that human suffering and alienation are caused by selfish attachment; and in the hope of ultimate liberation from the wheel of suffering?

To be sure, this would not be like the Christian way, but it would not be beyond the divine power to reveal some objective truth about ultimate reality and the self-sacrificial way to liberation, that took the faithful beyond self-centred and arbitrary ideas and practices. In which case the characterisation of religion as always arbitrary and wilful would be unfair and unduly pessimistic. Barth modified his position later, especially in *Dogmatics*, volume IV, part 3, but still did not allow that truths other than the Christian could be more than echoes or analogies of Christian truth. It is hard to see how he could hold both that religions are arbitrary and wilful and that the Holy Spirit is or has been at work in Judaism and in other religions too. It might seem that he would have to say that religions are partly arbitrary and sinful and partly touched by the Holy Spirit, and therefore partly good and holy.

The revelation of Jesus Christ would no longer be opposed to religion, and it would no longer make Christianity the 'true religion' in any sense other than that it is believed by its followers to affirm more important truths than are present in any other religion.

Interpretations of Revelation

If in more than one religion there can be true, even if incomplete, beliefs, it is also the case that many possible interpretations exist of exactly what propositional beliefs follow from the specifically Christian revelatory experience of Jesus Christ. Is the Spirit divine or just sent from God? Even after forgiveness, is there some penalty to be paid for grievous sin? Are only those who have such an experience liberated from sin? Is it possible to fall away from commitment to God? All these questions, and many others, were to become the source of centuries of debate and arguments, sometimes shamefully violent, in the churches.

Many questions about the truth-content of God's revelation remain unanswered by the description of God's revelation which Barth suggests. There are different ways of understanding divine judgment and grace, and Barth's beliefs about such things as pre-destination, the fall, the Trinity, and the Atonement are only one set of Protestant beliefs. They are highly contested even by those who hold to a high view of Biblical revelation. I agree with Barth on some of those matters, and disagree with him on others. I would find it objectionable and irrational to be told that Barth's beliefs were those of God, whereas mine were just made up by me.

We just have to decide between different interpretations of Biblical texts as best as we can. It is reasonable to hold that God's revelation, in the form of true propositions, may certainly be found in the Bible. But it is very hard to decide, for example, purely by reading Biblical propositions, whether God will save all humans, or only some humans (it is hard to decide even what Barth thinks on this issue). I therefore doubt whether it can be honestly said that God's revelation is clearly and completely given in the writings of the Bible, and nowhere else. Even in the Bible, the truth is very difficult to discern, as is shown by the fact that different believers, even the most devout, discern it in different ways.

What this means is that when it comes to saying what the content of God's revelation is, human reasoning, decision-making, and interpretation inevitably play a large part. There is no possibility of making a clear distinction between what God communicates and what human reasoning apprehends. To that extent it is misleading to distinguish sharply between human religion and divine revelation, and to be sure that one can identify what one is inclined to believe with exactly what God desires to disclose. It looks as if 'sublimation' cannot consist, as Barth says it does, in God's revelation cancelling and yet fulfilling human religion. There just have to be human choices about religious truth and religious 'revelations'. The appeal to God's direct revelation, which is what Barth seems to mean by 'sublimation', turns out to be no more than a subjective certainty that one's own belief choice is correct.

Barth defended recognisably Protestant doctrines of total and radical human sinfulness and God's free decision to forgive and sanctify (some or all?) humans without any consideration of their merit. These very severe doctrines, which I for one do not accept, are and are intended to be in opposition to the theological interpretations of many other theologians of his culture, which is precisely why he wrote the *Church Dogmatics*.

In other words, he stands in a particular tradition of Christian thought, the Evangelical Protestant tradition. Even within that tradition, he aims to set it in a new direction, to provide new insights into what Christian faith is.

In fact his theology is quite well described as a sublimation of the general Catholic tradition, cancelling the Catholic emphasis on penance and good works, yet fulfilling in a new way the Catholic insistence on the efficacy of the work of Christ and the Spirit. In this sense, German liberal theologians had also intended to sublimate many orthodox Protestant beliefs. They cancelled doctrines of the inerrancy of Scripture, the necessity of faith in Jesus for salvation, and the existence of eternal Hell. They intended to fulfil and transform the doctrines of the presence of the Spirit in the hearts of men and women, of the universal Fatherhood of God, and of the categorical demands of love. This is a meaningful sense of sublimation.

It is very different from Barth's sense, which is extremely paradoxical. The paradox is clear. All religions, Barth says, including Christianity, are failed human attempts to find God. As failures, they are obviously false. Yet he says that (one version of) Christianity is true. That is a plain contradiction, not a profound truth. Barth means by sublimation that what is cancelled is religion devised by human beings, which he calls a religion of works–righteousness. What is fulfilled is religion which is given by God, who chooses and forgives and sanctifies without any regard to human merit or moral endeavour. But if the divine choice is really without any regard for human attributes or merits, there is no reason why God should not choose and forgive members of many or even of all religions, however mistaken they are.

The Misleading Use of Sublimation

Sublimation, the generation of a new understanding out of previous partial understandings, does not after all seem a wholly appropriate term for what Barth has in mind.

If the term sublimation is used, there must be something that is retained and fulfilled, though it is also changed by a balancing element. That implies that there is something good, not wholly sinful, that can be taken into a new understanding. That in turn suggests a more positive account of any religion which can be fulfilled (sublimated), and not just rejected. And that may be true of many religions – it was certainly true of Judaism, before it rejected Christ. Many religions have elements which could be cancelled and many others that could be fulfilled, and so they could be sublimated. It is hard to see how Christianity, as a religion, is markedly different from many other religions, except perhaps that it has fewer elements to cancel (for Roman Catholics, the existence of limbo, perhaps?) and more to preserve and fulfil (God's extension of salvation to non-Catholics?). And that, really, is a matter of degree. Ironically, it takes one back to the 'liberal' claim that Christianity is the highest form of religion.

However, Barth still insists that the Christian religion is the only true one (I am allowing, for the moment, that calling religions true or false makes sense). In fact he would be worse than the liberals, because he would hold, not that Christian faith was just a superior religion in some important respects, but that it alone was true. As Tom Greggs, an eminent defender of Barth, puts it, Jesus is not just 'the pinnacle of God's works', as if he is the greatest spiritual teacher among others. Jesus is 'the source from which all other works of God are derived'.[8] Unfortunately, that gives Jesus total superiority over any other spiritual teachers. That may be true, but it is not significantly different from saying that the religion which follows Jesus is superior to all others.

Even worse, Barth might mean that (his version of) Christianity is sublimated in the totally different sense that God just chooses to accept a specific set of humans belonging to a particular religion, while their religion remains self-serving and arbitrary. That seems a peculiarly arbitrary and unjust decision by God – though I accept that this judgment touches on a centuries-old dispute about whether justification is predestined and imputed by God alone or requires human co-operation and endeavour. There are weighty theological decisions at stake here. The point is that they are decisions. God does not seem to have decided such matters for us.

I conclude that what Barth calls 'the revelation of God' is no more than what Barth *believes* to be the revelation of God. Christian religion is, after all, a religion like any other. Nothing changes in its content when Barth says it is sublimated. He only means that God is really active in revelation there, and nowhere else. There is no explicit statement of such a mean-spirited view, either in the Bible or anywhere else.

The term 'sublimation' is not really appropriate to the Christian religion, since the beliefs in the Spirit, grace, sin, and sanctification which are supposed to be the results of sublimation have been there from the first. There is no need to fulfil or transcend them. The concept of sublimation, of being cancelled in one form but fulfilled or transcended in another form, does not really apply.

Finally, religion is not wholly a matter of attempts by man to justify himself or develop a wilful and arbitrary idea of God. These ideas are simply not of interest to many of the world religions. Where religions are concerned with judgment and reconciliation

---

[8] Tom Greggs, *Theology against Religion* (London: T. and T. Clark, 2011), p. 178.

(as in Judaism and Islam, for instance), there is little reason to deny that a God of judgment and reconciliation really is active in them, as their adherents believe. I cannot see any reason for this denial, apart from a stubborn and wholly unevidenced insistence that humans, and all human activities, are totally sinful. Barth supported his view by inventing extreme and imaginary oppositions between religion and revelation, faith and certainty, human total sinfulness and overwhelming divine grace. I think it is of the first importance to show decisively why the teaching of Barth in this section of the *Church Dogmatics* is fundamentally flawed. It is even, as Barth said of the views of people like me, 'an actual heresy'.

5 | Revelation against Religion

Analysis of Barth's First Chapter: 'The Problem of Religion in Theology'

I shall now move on to consider the three chapters which comprise the body of Barth's discussion of religion.

Barth begins his discussion of religion with the assertion that revelation cannot be understood as some sort of interplay between God and man, as though God reveals, but the possibility of receiving this revelation lies in man. It is God who makes it possible for man to hear revelation. It is not an innate human possibility.

He makes it clear, however, that he is speaking only of Christian revelation, for, as he goes on to say, there is a human possibility of relating to a higher Spirit, 'something ultimate and decisive' in many religions (41). Even the idea of 'one sole and supreme God' is present in some religions. There is in fact 'a sea ... of parallels and analogies' to Christian beliefs in the world religions. There is a human possibility and actuality for religion in many human societies.

Thereby Barth begins to establish a relationship – a wholly misleading one, as it turns out – between 'religion' as a human phenomenon and 'revelation' as an act of God. He then holds that Christianity is, uniquely, both a human phenomenon and an act of revelation by God.

The real question, he says, is whether revelation should be explained and interpreted by religion, or whether religion should be explained and interpreted by revelation. The problem with this question is that it is utterly misconceived. Barth has invented something he calls 'religion', which covers all the religions of the world. Then he has invented something he calls 'revelation', which is an act of God which creates a new and unprecedented possibility for receiving what God says 'in judgment and grace'.

Barth rightly says that 'religion', used as a general descriptive term, is a fairly new invention. Wilfred Cantwell Smith's book, *The Meaning and End of Religion*, argues that 'the concept of religion is recent, Western-and-Islamic, and unstable'.[1] Cantwell Smith hopes that the term would 'have disappeared from serious writing and careful speech within twenty five years',[2] though by using the term in the title of his book he ensured that it would continue to be used!

He distinguishes between cumulative traditions, which differ in many ways in accordance with the histories and customs of diverse cultures, and personal faith in a transcendent divine reality, which is, he thinks, common to all humans. This sounds similar to what Barth does, but in fact it is almost the opposite. For Cantwell Smith, since there is no such thing as religion, there is nothing which is inherently wilful and arbitrary, and there is nothing to sublimate. Personal faith, on the other hand, is not confined to any culture or tradition, and Christian faith in the judgment and mercy of God is just one among many ways of relating to transcendent reality.

On this view, revelation could not be explained by religion, because 'religion' is a reification that is so misleading that it should not be used at all. We can, to be sure, speak of particular cumulative traditions, but each one is different, and if they are considered, they should be considered in their specific particularity, not as similar members of some identifiable general species. The general term 'religion' is not like a Platonic universal in which all particular religions share. It is more like a collection or bundle of variously

---

[1] Wilfred Cantwell Smith, *The Meaning and End of Religion* (London: Macmillan, 1962), p. 120.
[2] Ibid., p. 195.

related and overlapping forms of life (this is sometimes called a 'bundle' view of collective nouns, and it, though not the word, is attributed to Wittgenstein).

I cannot see how a study of various religious traditions could be used as an explanation of revelation. Some traditions do not use the concept at all; others use it in a number of different senses; Barth's peculiar use of it to mean, apparently, a divine act without any human co-operation, is one of them. Having said that, what sort of explanation has been given of revelation? The study of religions does not lay down any rules for what could count as a revelation; it merely says what counts as revelation in various traditions, and as such makes no judgment about its usefulness or truth.

Each particular religion, or cumulative tradition, to use Cantwell Smith's term, must be understood from within, so that what is said about it must be acceptable to an adherent of that tradition, whether or not the researcher agrees with it. If, for instance, you seek to understand Hinduism from within, that might expand your understanding of how human life can be seen in different ways, of how your view can be seen by others, and of what the strengths and weaknesses of both Hinduism and your own position are. It can be an enrichment of understanding, and it may increase your tolerance of and sympathy with others. Sometimes, of course, it may strengthen your opposition to a view you study, and give you more informed reasons for rejecting it (that is what happens to me when I read Barth).

So a study of religions may affect your view of revelation. But this is not letting 'religion' dictate what 'revelation' is. As Cantwell Smith says, 'religion' is a very vague, multidimensional term that does not refer to one easily identifiable entity. A study of religions may affect what you think, but it will not dictate what you can think, or suggest any definitive idea of revelation as true.

What is considered as the study of religions (and I was the Professor of the History of Religion at King's College, London University for some years) is, or should be, the study in depth of some particular religious traditions (it is not possible to study all of them, even in a lifetime), and sometimes, but not always, the analysis of similarities to or parallels with other traditions, and differences between them. 'Religion', despite what Cantwell Smith said, continues to be a useful general term to mark off a specific area of research – namely, human concerns with spiritual reality or realities. But it is a mistake to reify the term 'religion' and use it as though it referred to some entity that could be used to explain something. The study of religious traditions does not provide or even suggest a criterion of truth. It is essentially descriptive and pluralistic. It describes what people think, feel, and do, and shows how diverse, yet often overlapping, religious traditions are. While the concept of 'revelation' occurs in some such traditions, the student of religion should refrain from making judgments about whether specific alleged revelations provide propositions which are true.

Any student will, of course, have opinions about truth. When I taught religious studies, I thought many Christian assertions were true. But it was not my job to argue for their truth. It was my job to display, as well as I could, the reasons that could be offered for thinking specific religious beliefs true or false. I considered it wise to make my own beliefs clear, so that students could look out for any unconscious bias in my expositions. But there was nothing in the study of religions as such that could show that a specific view of revelation was actually correct.

Some, often sociologically or Marxist-influenced, scholars of religion do hold that only unbelievers can properly study religious phenomena, and understand them for what they really are – delusions arising out of social discomforts, perhaps. It is right, in religious studies, to mention such views, and also to criticise them. But it is not for the scholar of religions to decide on their truth.

This is admittedly a remark about the non-ideological teaching of religions. There are particular schools, both religious and secular, where one set of beliefs will be officially regarded as correct (there are Marxist and Roman Catholic schools). In the religious case, these would normally be called schools of theology, not religious studies. When Hans Kung was removed from his position in a Catholic school of theology, he simply transferred to a school of religious studies, and continued his distinguished academic career.

Karl Barth was a theologian, and so took it as his job to defend the beliefs of one section of the Protestant Christian church to which he belonged. I have no objection to that, though I think that theology has a much wider brief than that of defending the view of some brand of religion. When, after a few years as a professor of the history of religion, I became a professor of theology, which also involved being a canon in an Anglican cathedral, I did regard it as part of my job to defend a set of Christian beliefs. But I also saw theology as an academic study of beliefs about God, or more widely a study of beliefs about a spiritual reality or realities, in which people of many faiths or none could participate. Thus, theology is not necessarily Christian theology, though it does concern itself more with questions of religious truth than the discipline of religious studies.

The Relation between Revelation and Religion

If revelation cannot be explained by religion, since religions are diverse and the study of religions is primarily descriptive, could religion be explained by some particular revelation? Some theology schools, though not all, might try to do so. That is, they might try to assess religious claims assuming the truth of some revealed (or sometimes devastatingly secular) beliefs. In fact that is what Barth recommends, the beliefs he commends being those of his own denomination of Protestant Christianity. But to understand Hindu thought, for example, in terms of Christian revelation, is a guaranteed way to misunderstand it. If you are going to disagree with the beliefs of some religion, you should at least try to understand it in its own terms first. Only then can you say how your own tradition disagrees with it, and why. But disagreeing with a view does not mean that you understand it in terms of your own different view.

A good example is Christian views of Islam. If Islam is understood in terms of Christian revelation, it will be seen as a misunderstanding of the Gospel, a return to a religion of law and works, and a rejection of Jesus as Messiah. This would be a total misunderstanding of how Islam sees itself as a universal religion of total obedience to a God of mercy and compassion. Only when an attempt to gain an internal understanding of Islam has been made will it become acceptable to explore a Christian response to it. This should not be an understanding of Islam in terms of Christian revelation, seen as a God-given and unquestionable truth. It will be a point-by-point comparison of beliefs, perhaps with reasons given why Christians accept the Christian version.

It distorts both the study of religion and the study of Christian theology to say that either divine revelation should be understood in terms of some alleged general description of religions, or that religions should be understood in terms of just one divine revelation. There is no general description of religions that will entail a particular view of revelation. And there is no view of revelation that will, in itself, generate a fair description of all religions. One should understand each religion on its own terms, and if desired engage in a point-by-point discussion of where and why differences exist.

Universal Concepts of Religion

When Barth speaks about 'a universal concept of religion', he cannot be talking about the scholarly study of religions at all, which usually begins by denying that there is any agreed universal concept of religion. In fact it is Barth himself who comes nearest to propounding a universal concept of religion, when he remarks that the 'essence of religion' is faithlessness and sin. It is hard to know what could justify him in thinking that every religion is arbitrary and sinful. I think that one of the things he really has in mind is the impossibility of natural theology, that is, theology without revelation.

His very limited and one-sided survey of the history of Protestant religious thought sees that history as 'insidious', 'something unfortunate', 'destructive', 'catastrophic', and 'an actual heresy'. What actually happened, however, was almost exactly the opposite. It was the triumph of understanding over ignorance (though elements of a Western sense of superiority sometimes remained). Since the seventeenth century it became possible, for the first time, to have access to and study world religions, with close attention to what they were really saying about themselves. This was because of increased knowledge of other languages, increased access to original documents, and increased possibilities of travel to other cultures. It became clear that there were many types of revelation and authority in the world religions, and for the first time scholars were forced to take them seriously, and not simply discount them as demonic or primitive. That is a growth of knowledge and understanding, and it is infinitely preferable to the refusal of the earlier Protestant theologians to study non-Christian ways of faith altogether. This was a progress in understanding, not at all a catastrophe.

It was an expansion of knowledge also because, within the Christian world, there was a growing awareness of how discoveries in science raised problems for taking the Bible literally, how the overthrow of Aristotelian philosophy made many originally Greek philosophical terms used in theology, and derivates of them (like 'substance', 'accident', 'nature', and 'person') questionable, and how the development of critical historical methods led to greater knowledge of how the Biblical writings were pieced together and edited. These were developments both in religious studies and in theology.[3]

Barth's comments and his 'history' are both inventions of his own. What he seems to be really concerned with is the development of natural theology, constructed by reason and argument. This was a

---

[3] I have given a survey and assessment of how these post-Enlightenment movements impacted on theology in my *Religion in the Modern World*.

quite separate matter, though it was partly motivated by an attempt to resolve the contradictions between the different revelations that were alleged to have occurred. The best-known exponents of such a view are probably Kant and Hegel. Kant was not even a Christian, and Hegel, though claiming to be a Lutheran, is widely viewed as interpreting Christian religion as a sort of picture image of his own philosophy.

Barth may or may not be right about whether the attempt to prove God, freedom, and immortality by reason failed. Kant, it should be noted, thought that it did fail, though he appealed to faith (not the Christian faith) to remedy this. But this is not a development within Christian theology; it is an attempt to have a religion without revelation. There were such attempts, but they were always rather unusual, not very widely accepted, and do not in any way establish such a monstrosity as 'a universal concept of religion'. They are rather conscious attempts to 'sublimate' Christianity by a more rational faith – rather as Hegel's Absolute Idealism could be seen as sublimated Lutheranism.[4]

These notions of sublimation are more plausible than the one Barth unwisely attempts to use, which holds that just one religion is sublimated by God. That is a form of Evangelical Protestantism, and it does not appeal to reason or increased understanding of the diversity of human beliefs to argue for its truth. It is just assumed as self-evident to those, and only to those, who accept the Bible as the only revealed source of truth (a very peculiar definition of 'self-evident', since it is not accepted by millions of intelligent people). It even deplores any attempt to understand other forms of religious life – 'Revelation is understood only where the first and last word about religion is expected from it and it alone' (61). This extraordinary and clearly false statement alleges that we can know all about the world's religions, in all their complexity and variety,

---

[4] Though on this much-disputed subject see Hegel's *Lectures on the Philosophy of Religion*, and my discussion of Hegel in *Religion in the Modern World*.

by just thinking about the Christian revelation. There is nothing to learn from any other faith.

This again is a view he modified later, saying that we could listen to what other faiths say. Even then, however, he is looking for echoes of Christian truth in other places, not for genuinely new insights that are not found in most Christian theologies. He is seeing those other faiths in the light of the truth of Jesus Christ. That is an improvement on not paying any attention to them at all. But it is quite a long way from seeing them in their own terms.

I myself accept the Christian faith, but I would be appalled to learn that God had nothing of any interest to reveal in any other faith, or that I could not learn more about my own faith by learning anything from other faiths. On the contrary, I believe I have learned more from Buddhism about universal compassion for all life than I can find in the main Christian tradition. I have learned more about the possibility of union with God from Hinduism than I have learned from many forms of Protestant Christianity. And there are many other things to be learned. To suppose that there are no such things, when one has not even made the attempt to find out, is a form of culpable ignorance.

Uncertainties in Revelation

If we are Christians, we should know that we have the possibility and actuality of knowing God. But does this tell us that nobody but us has such a possibility? Is my faith such that it forbids me to say that others too can have a genuine faith given to them by the supreme spiritual reality, which I believe to be God? Well, it may be said, other faiths differ from mine, so from my point of view they make mistakes, and therefore cannot be true revelations. But do I never make mistakes in my faith? Have I never been wrong in the things I believe? I know I have made mistakes. But I do believe that God reveals himself to me, even if I think the Heidelberg Catechism, to which Barth often appeals, is not completely correct.

Barth says that my faith must be certain; I must be certain of it; whereas all those people who talk about 'religion' must always be subject to doubt and uncertainty. Therefore they lack true faith. 'Uncertainty in the conception of revelation ... means lack of faith' (58). This seems to me to misunderstand completely what faith means. Faith is trust. You trust someone when you cannot be certain they will do as they say, but you may still in the right circumstances stake your life on it.

Where you have knowledge, you do not need faith. I do not have faith that I see a red patch in front of me. I just know it because of what I see now. This is a simple perception, and nobody will contest it. But knowing God is knowing something that is conceptually very complex, and it is highly contested by intelligent and informed people. For instance, some people think that God is an omnipotent, omniscient, and perfectly good being. Others think that God is a God of somewhat limited power, knowledge, and goodness. Can a simple perception decide between these alternatives? Can it possibly make it certain that what we perceive is an omnipotent being? That does not seem possible. It seems very unlikely, therefore, that an alleged apprehension of God could be in itself certain knowledge. If I have faith that there is a gracious God, I am similarly committing myself to something of which I logically cannot be certain.

In the case of trust in humans, I must have some reason for my faith in you. It would not be heroic or praiseworthy, it would be absurd, to trust someone of whom you know nothing. If the unknown person said, 'I am completely trustworthy', that would not help. Why should we trust that statement, which may easily be made by a rogue? The character and previous conduct of the person are relevant and desirable, even necessary, if trust is to be appropriate.

In the case of an alleged religious revelation, we must have some reasons for thinking that there is a revealer and that the revealer is worth trusting. At the very least, we would want to know that the revelation is consistent, morally acceptable, compatible with well-established knowledge of the world, and that it has good historical provenance.

By such criteria many critics have found Biblical revelation problematic. They claim that in the Bible there are inconsistencies, morally dubious passages (like the command to exterminate the Canaanites),[5] problems about six-day creation and the age of the universe, and questions about the historical reliability of some documents. They have not been led to see these problems by lack of faith, though some critics have found them severe enough to cause them to lose faith. Those like me, who keep faith, have to admit that there are problems, but we think that solutions can be found, if only by reformulating some traditional beliefs. Solutions in my case involve denying the total inerrancy of Scripture, and accepting that revelation is always qualified by limited human reception, while continuing to hold that it contains a genuine revelation of God's judgment and mercy, the Incarnation and Lordship of Jesus Christ, and the promise of eternal life. Though there may be relatively unimportant contradictions, for instance in the dating of the Last Supper in different Gospels,[6] there is, more importantly, the revelation of God in the life of a human person, the idea of God as suffering and unlimited love, and the hope for all of sharing in the divine nature. Even these distinctive beliefs of Christian revelation are not theoretically certain – they are very complex and widely contested. They too involve total commitment to the objectively uncertain.

That is absolutely opposed to Barth's view. He writes, 'Revelation is denied whenever it is treated as problematic' (63). Yet all claims to revelation from God are problematic, whether they are Jewish,

---

[5] Deuteronomy 20, 10–18.
[6] Compare 'On the first day of Unleavened Bread' (Mark 26, 17) and 'Before the Feast of the Passover' (John 13, 1).

Muslim, or Christian. He calls views like mine 'demonic', and insists that it is just lack of faith not to accept the Heidelberg Catechism as axiomatic and unquestionable (59). Yet despite this he claims that in his theology there is 'the free investigation of truth' (58). I, for my part, think Barth does not know what the free investigation of truth means. Any free investigation must at least recognise that other people see problems with the Heidelberg Catechism (I do, for a start). Problems do arise with faith, new ones in each generation.

Problems with revelation arise from within the revealed religions themselves, as new knowledge of the world throws doubt on many traditional assertions. To say that we must treat such traditional assertions as axiomatic when they are widely challenged, both within and outside the Christian faith, is to forbid the free investigation of truth. The fact is that the best way to pursue truth is to take every criticism seriously, and be prepared to respond to new information as it arises.

Even if we start with Scripture, we soon find ourselves asking: do demons cause disease, and could they really talk to Jesus? Was there a Garden of Eden? Will Jesus return soon? Did God really tell the Israelites to wipe out the Amalekites? These problems arise within this tradition. They cause many to look to medical science, to cosmology, to biological evolution, to critical history, to gender studies, and to the ancient Greek philosophical background of many of the key terms of Christian doctrine, to test claims seemingly made in Scripture against the assured findings of modern science. In view of this, it seems inaccurate to say that Scriptural revelation should be immune from the criticisms or even the influence of reason, and that it should just be accepted on its own terms.

Barth thinks that the Bible should be the primary if not the sole source of religious beliefs (though he also apparently accepts the Heidelberg Confession as authoritative), because it is the Word of God. So the Biblical revelation is the test against which all religions must be judged. 'The universal', he says, 'is sublimated by the particular.' That is, religions are all human, sinful constructions. But they – or in fact just one of them, the Protestant – are cancelled in their sinfulness and transformed into truth by the gracious action of God. The others remain sinful, self-centred, and wilful.

This is an extraordinarily insensitive judgment. Muslims would say that God, a God of judgment and compassion, acts to reveal and be present in Islam. In fact Islam could very plausibly be said to sublimate Christianity, since it comes after Christianity, cancels the doctrine of Incarnation, but fulfils the doctrine of revelation by having words dictated by God in person, and in perfect Arabic, not second-hand records in often rather poor Greek of what Jesus said, probably in Aramaic.

Christians, of course, would not agree. But they would have to give reasons, which might include testimony to the resurrection of Jesus, acceptance of the need for a redeemer to reconcile the world to God, and the danger in Islam of violent and intolerant interpretations of jihad. But in justice Christians would have to accept that Muslims would have reasons for rejecting Christian beliefs – maybe that the testimonies to the resurrection are weak, that the idea of a human who is divine is a form of idolatry, that no redeemer is necessary for God to forgive sin, and that Christianity has been as violent and intolerant as Islam.

Revelation and Interpretation

If a Christian sees that there are reasons for rejecting claims to divine revelation, a Christian would in all fairness have to accept that there are reasons for not accepting the Bible as given by God, and they would therefore have to be able to respond by giving reasons for accepting the authority of Scripture. These reasons include appeal to: the reliability of human observation and testimony, on the part of the first disciples, for example; assessments of human nature as inherently sinful or not; the moral consequences of belief;

and questions about the coherence of an alleged revelation with other well-accepted human knowledge.

A good guide is what is sometimes called the Wesleyan Quadrilateral,[7] which states that there are four main sources of Christian or in fact of any religious belief – revelation, personal experience, tradition, and reason. Appeal to revelation is appeal to some authoritative teaching, usually a written text. Some people will take a text as inerrant, but others will allow for social and cultural factors that must be taken into account, while finding the basic teaching of the text to be a genuine communication from a god or teacher with superior access to spiritual truth.

As a Christian, I trust the New Testament records of the life and teaching of Jesus, who is seen as having supreme access to spiritual truth, as being very reliable, but I do not think they are inerrant.

What we might call the 'revelation of Jesus Christ' is in fact the end-product of a chain of elements, from the experience of Jesus himself, the disciples' personal perceptions of Jesus' life and teaching, the oral circulation of these perceptions in the early churches, the edited accounts of some of these memories in four Gospels with rather different points of view, and later translations of and commentaries on New Testament texts which were written in Greek.

We do not have direct access to Jesus, though there are many present experiences which Christians interpret as being of a living and risen Jesus. These tend to corroborate the New Testament records, but it would be only natural to think that there might remain many differences of viewpoint and interpretation in what we may call the revelation of Jesus in the Bible.

Nevertheless, it is very clear that Jesus was believed by his disciples to be the Messiah, the Christ. He preached repentance, and the forgiveness of sins. He taught that the kingdom or rule of God had

---

[7] A term allegedly founded on the works of John Wesley, but first propounded by the twentieth-century American Methodist scholar Albert Outley.

come near, and that he was anointed by the Spirit to bring good news to the poor.[8]

Barth felt that one should begin, in theology, with this simple Gospel of the forgiveness of sins, the gift of the Holy Spirit, and the hope of eternal life. It was a mistake to begin theology with a generalised definition of religion (like Schleiermacher's 'sense of the Infinite' or Otto's '*mysterium tremendum et fascinans*'), and then find the Christian Gospel as the best case of such a definition. We do not need to seek after some general definition of religious consciousness.

In setting out a theology, however, one must set out what the Messiah is, what the kingdom of God is, and what the Holy Spirit is. One cannot do that without explaining how these terms – Messiah, God's kingdom, and Holy Spirit – originated and developed. It will turn out that these key ideas are not clearly and definitively defined in the New Testament. It took many years, and many arguments, before the Messiah became seen as the divine Word of God (as opposed to the Arian view that Jesus was not quite divine), God's kingdom became widely interpreted as the fellowship of the redeemed in Christ (not as a cataclysmic divine ending of human history in the near future), and the Holy Spirit was said to be one 'person' or aspect of a Trinitarian God (as opposed to a Spirit sent from, but not identical with, God).

The revelation of Jesus Christ is not one certain and unanimously agreed thing. Barth himself belongs to one, Reformed, tradition of interpretation, which differs in important ways from Catholic and Orthodox beliefs, and even from other Reformed theologians like Schleiermacher. If he did not, he would not have written the *Church Dogmatics*.

When Barth speaks of the revelation of Jesus Christ, he is therefore speaking of what he believes to be revealed about God by the figure of Jesus that is presented in the New Testament. Jesus, Barth thinks,

---

[8] Luke 4, 18–22.

has to be seen as the historical exemplar, the temporal Incarnation, of the eternal Christ who was present at creation and in whom all things in the universe will finally be united.[9] The risen Jesus, existing in a very different spiritual form from that which he had on earth,[10] will continue to mediate the eternal Christ to humanity. But there are different interpretations of what Jesus shows about God. One is that he shows a God of severe judgment, who, on a terrifying Day of the Lord, will send many to be punished for their sins. Christ is appointed as the judge who will divide the righteous and faithful from the wicked and faithless.[11] Another is that he shows God's unlimited and universal love, which will bring everyone to fellowship with God. Christ is one who takes on himself all judgment due to humans, and unites them all – and all things in Heaven and earth – to God.[12]

Barth seems to take the latter interpretation, seeing Jesus not as a severe judge who condemns many but as one who shows the universal and unlimited love of God. What Barth takes to be a distinctive and unique revelation of Jesus Christ is in fact based on his personal selection from the New Testament narratives. This selection is one that most traditional interpretations of the Bible reject. It seems that what Barth thinks of as the revelation of Jesus Christ turns out to be one minority interpretation of Biblical writings. This is hardly an appeal to a revelation from God rather than a human religious interpretation.

If so, revelation is not, as the work of Barth seems to imply, a direct act of God which stands in some opposition to the tortuous

---

[9] See Colossians 1, 15–20: 'In him were all things created ... and through him God was pleased to reconcile to himself all things, whether on earth or in Heaven.'

[10] 'What we will be has not yet been revealed ... when he is revealed we will be like him' (1 John 3, 2). This entails that we do not know the form of the glorified Christ.

[11] Matthew 25, 31–2: 'When the Son of Man comes in his glory ... all the nations will be gathered before him, and he will separate people one from another as a shepherd separates the sheep from the goats.'

[12] Ephesians 1, 9–10: 'He has made known to us the mystery of his will ... to gather up all things in him, things in Heaven and things on earth.'

and diverse processes of religion by which interpretations of revelation are formulated. Similar processes of selection and interpretation occur in many major religions, so that it is not something
quite unique to Christianity. Many faiths have their revelations or
authoritative teachings, and there is no reason why Barth's own
faith should possess the distinction of being sublimated into something uniquely God-given and uniquely true.

Why should it be true that human reflection and imagination
will always be opposed to revelation, whereas one, and only one,
religious authority (the Bible) should provide objective truth and
succeed in describing what God is really like? The answer to that
question requires investigation of various opposing religious
claims. That will be part of theology proper, and it is important that
it be undertaken seriously and sensitively. It cannot be said that
Barth does this.

The Wesleyan Quadrilateral

I have considered the first element of the Wesleyan Quadrilateral,
revelation. The other three elements of the Wesleyan Quadrilateral
are personal experience, tradition, and reason.

Appeal to personal experience is appeal to a person's own
acquaintance with a spiritual presence and power, or trust in such
experiences of others. Some will take vivid personal experiences as
definitive, while others will allow that their interpretations of experience will be culturally and historically conditioned, though the
experiences themselves will be compelling. I believe I experience
the presence of the Holy Spirit and of the risen Christ, but I allow
that I may make mistakes as I try to interpret them more fully.[13]

Appeal to tradition is a matter of seeing how religious traditions have been developed over the years, and how informed

---

[13] A good treatment of this topic is Caroline Franks Davis, *The Evidential Force of
Religious Experience* (Oxford: Clarendon Press, 1989).

commentators have shaped traditions. Some will take a specific commentator as finally authoritative, but others will allow that all human writers make mistakes and have their own prejudices, even though there are writers who can give insights one might not have obtained by oneself. My thoughts have certainly been shaped by such writers as Augustine, Aquinas, Macquarrie, and Hick, whom I take to be illuminating commentators on the Christian tradition. But I have developed my own personal views, which would not have existed without them, yet which do not slavishly follow any of them.[14]

Appeal to reason involves seeing how far religious teachings motivate, or are consistent with, knowledge obtained from the sciences and from the humanities. Some will think that religious beliefs are superior to and may often oppose any secular knowledge, but others think that they need to conform with the best independently established knowledge, particularly in the sciences and morality. I accept all well-established scientific facts like evolution and cosmology, and the main moral advances of the Enlightenment like gender equality, human autonomy, and human rights, and adapt traditional Christian beliefs in the light of this new knowledge. This is quite compatible with accepting the reality of the spiritual realm, and the unique place of Jesus in manifesting and mediating this realm.[15]

It is clear that these tests will not provide unanimously agreed approaches to religion, and that they are not capable of providing theoretical certainty. Religious beliefs will therefore always remain diverse and to a certain extent theoretically tentative. Any individual begins from a specific attitude to them, and all one can hope is that people should seek to reflect on their learned beliefs, and seek the widest range of views they can, while trying to discriminate the reasonable from the unreasonable. It is unlikely, in most cases, that

---

[14] My own account of the development of Christian traditions can be found in *Re-thinking Christianity* (London: Oneworld, 2007).

[15] I have written an account of the relation between scientific inquiry and Christian faith in *Pascal's Fire* (London: Oneworld, 2006) and in *God, Chance, and Necessity* (London: Oneworld, 1996).

fundamental beliefs will change completely, but they may certainly be expanded and deepened by reasoned, critical, and charitable reflection. It is quite possible, and indeed necessary, to make an absolute practical commitment to a spiritual path, while admitting theoretical uncertainty about many of its claims. That is just the human condition, in many if not most human realms of human endeavour.

A Christian cannot therefore deny the importance of reasoning about whether a certain Scripture is given by God or not. In a sense the Bible and the beliefs it contains must be subject to moral, experiential, and rational criticism. Barth seems to fear that this would be to subject God and God's Word to some superior criterion of reason, something superior to God. But that is clearly not the case. What is being criticised is a *human claim* to know what God is, and to know what God has revealed in the Bible. This is not a criticism of God, but of human claims. Even the much vaunted 'inner testimony of the Holy Spirit' is in fact a human claim that there is a Holy Spirit which makes me sure of something. Even if it is true (as I believe it is) that the Holy Spirit gives one spiritual assurance and faith, the claim that this is so is a claim made by some limited and fallible human intellect. Human claims are always subject to critical inquiry, for we know that they are often mistaken, and it is vital to find out if they are correct, especially when they make such world-shaking claims that are denied by so many.

What Barth refuses to admit is that critical study of the Christian revelation is not criticism of God or of God's truth. It is criticism of fallible human claims made by people who say that they know what God and God's truth are. There is no evading this fact. It completely undermines Barth's claim that there is a revelation of God which is absolutely certain and free of any criticism.

6 | The Failure of Religion

Analysis of Barth's Second Chapter: 'Religion as Faithlessness'

Barth begins the second chapter of the *Church Dogmatics* by claiming that all religions are opposed to and condemned by God. He radically opposes 'God's grace over against all world religion' (68). Religion is not a path to God, but 'in religion man resists and closes himself off to revelation' (75). He does not hesitate to make such a pronouncement about *all* world religions, when it is most unlikely that he, or anyone, could know enough about all world religions to see whether the comment was true.

What lies behind this provocative statement is his particular interpretation of humanity as 'unrighteous and unholy, and as such damned and lost' (83). This is a form of Christianity which takes a very low view of humans. He says that 'in relation to God every act is in vain' (73). Every act of man is condemned by God, however good it might seem. This opinion, which I as a Christian by no means share, has the consequence that if every act is vain, then so is the act of believing that God in Christ has redeemed the world. The Christian faith itself, considered as a number of acts of believing, must be vain. The only hope of avoiding this conclusion is that this religion, or at least some of the basic beliefs of this religion, are not from man, but directly from God. However, having said that all religious beliefs are vain, the belief that some proposition comes directly from God (which is, of course, a human belief) sounds an even greater product of human vanity than most other religious assertions. It is thus one of the least believable assertions that could be made.

Nevertheless, Barth is determined to take his stand on the truth of his version of the Christian religion as a fundamental presupposition. I understand the feeling that every treatment of religion must start from some initial attitude, and that it may seem unfair not to allow a Christian presupposition to be a reasonable starting point. He objects to what he thinks of as the liberal attitude that humans can stand as dispassionate observers of the world religions, and use pure reason to decide which one is correct. Such people, he says, would be 'enlightened know-it-alls' (69). He means people like Hegel or Kant, among the most eminent philosophers, who, he claims, use pure reason to decide what is right.

He objects to the process of looking at religions as human phenomena, discerning their key concepts and characteristics, and then finding that Christianity is the most advanced or superior religion. He finds that sort of adjudication between religions a matter of finding human reason capable of replacing faith, and of discriminating between religions as if from an unbiased standpoint. But that is an unfair characterisation of what usually happens.

We have all learned from an early age the beliefs or unbeliefs that we have been taught by adults we trust. Many of us stay with these beliefs throughout life. But many discover that there are grave problems with the beliefs we have been taught. These are specific problems that arise in a particular culture, not usually abstract theological points. People come across different beliefs, and it is likely that the wider their knowledge the more chance there is of seeing new or alternative possibilities. They adjust their views accordingly, but they probably never escape the general attitudes and dispositions to think in certain ways with which they have been born.

There is no guarantee of correctness, and the adoption of a view is not aptly described as a decision, so much as a dawning feeling that something is right or good. For the religious, this can be felt as a 'calling', but it has to be admitted that people feel very different callings from each other, and they are not all compatible. It is almost never a matter of 'pure reason', and usually a matter of feeling and intuition. Reasoning comes into it, of course, but it is rarely the only decisive element – the situation is more like being attracted to another person. We cannot help it, though it is wise to make some investigations before we make a firm commitment.

Barth writes as though liberal religious people have some idea of an 'essence of religion', which is a standard for comparing various religions, and then deciding by reason alone which is superior. That is wholly unrealistic. Some people may hear the Christian Gospel of sin, forgiveness, and resurrection, and feel the power of the Spirit moving them to belief. But others may hear the recitation of the Qur'an, and feel that Allah moves them to submit to his Word. Neither response is purely rational, or self-interested, or felt to be a response to a purely human construction. Neither can be guaranteed as correct, but it is not a matter of bare choice between abstract doctrines. It is a matter of feeling the strength and beauty of possibilities which are relevant and illuminating in one's own situation.

It is actually a form of slander to say that 'religion puts an image of God that man has wilfully and arbitrarily devised for himself' (79). To say that of a Muslim who aims to submit to the image of God that was revealed in the Qur'an is to accuse that Muslim of bad faith and hypocrisy. Who is Barth to make such a judgment? Such a thing is quite contrary to the teaching of Jesus that we should not judge others,[1] for only God knows the secrets of human hearts, and whether they are hypocritical or sincere. In any case, if I feel that it is true that the Holy Spirit is speaking to me, this does not at all imply that people of other faiths are all wilful and arbitrary (73). It may imply that they are mistaken in some respects, but that mistake is often quite intelligible, and is not at all connected with whether they have any idea about 'an essence of religion' or not.

---

[1] Matthew 7, 1: 'Do not judge, so that you may not be judged.'

Revelation and Diversity

The real question is how anyone can be certain that what they believe is truly given by God, and not just a personal fantasy. Different Christians, and different churches, give different answers to this question. Roman Catholics think that the Magisterium, the teaching authority of the church, and in particular the pope when speaking *ex cathedra*, can tell us. The Orthodox think that the definitions of the Ecumenical Councils can tell us. Many Protestants think that the Bible can tell us – but they do not agree whose interpretation of the Bible we should follow.

In view of all these differences, it seems silly to say that it ought to be clearly and certainly known by all what is truly revealed by God. Believers can say truthfully that there are a number of Christian views, and one must presumably accept one of them, but one should allow that the chosen view may be wrong. This is faith (trust in a particular authority), but it is a reasonable faith (though not the only reasonable one).

If my Christian faith includes the proposition that God is good and loving, it ought to add that God will accept even mistaken Christian views, as long as their holders mean to be obedient to Jesus Christ. If we go so far, it would surely not presume on God's love too much to say that God will accept non-Christian views also if, though mistaken, they aim for the best and most rational and life-giving view that they know. In other words, revelation is not confined, as it is in Barth's analysis, to one minority section of the Christian churches.

Barth later did later allow some sort of revelation to occur in spheres outside the Christian church, but he only allowed truths which already agreed at least in part with Christian revelations to count. I am suggesting that even within the Christian sphere, revelation is given in such a way that a diversity of interpretations is almost certain to arise. If that is the case, it seems that revelation is best understood as allowing or even inviting elements of dispute and diversity. It will not be a matter of dictating a set of clear doctrines which all the faithful must humbly accept. It will rather be the provision of a set of insights that provoke thought and invite the exploration of new ways of understanding. That entails that revelation is not a complete and changeless body of propositions, received 'pure and unadulterated' by humans. It is given by God as rather like a set of signposts for creative thought. Many human limitations and misperceptions may be linked with it, though its purpose is to give rise to new insights and perceptions.

A simple example of this might be the way in which slavery is never explicitly condemned in the Bible. By reflection on what is said about the dignity of all humans and the importance of human freedom, it has come to be thought by the vast majority of Christians that slavery is anti-Christian. Much the same may be said about the equality of men and women, which is not explicitly commanded in Scripture, and which is still contested by some Bible-believing Christians, but which the example of Jesus is widely thought to support.

In that case, there will be no absolute dividing line between 'religion' and 'revelation', as though one was purely and exclusively human (and therefore would exclude God's contribution) and the other was purely and exclusively divine (excluding any contribution by the receiver of revelation). That would destroy Barth's paradoxical contrast of a revelation-rejecting religion and a completely certain and wholly true divine revelation. It would remove the complex apparatus of simultaneous condemnation and justification, and replace it with the idea of revelation as involving 'an interplay between God and man, grace and nature' (39), which is everything Barth means to oppose.

Barth's paradox is that Christianity is both true and false, both condemned and forgiven. He does not exempt Christianity from the general condemnation of religion. He says 'religion is faithlessness' is a proposition 'aimed not only at various others with

their religion, but rather first of all at ourselves as members of
the Christian religion. It formulates the judgment of divine revelation upon all religion' (70). So the Christian religion, together
with all other religions, stands under the judgment of God. Yet he
thinks the Christian religion is also, at the same time, the object
of God's forgiveness and sanctification. As such, it must be true.
He thus locks himself into the self-contradictory assertion that
Christianity is both false (as a human religion) and true (as genuine divine revelation). This is a totally unnecessary move. The
obvious alternative is to say that if there is one correct religion,
Christianity, and if a number of religions are very like it, and even
share some beliefs with it, one can after all compare religions by
seeing how close to Christianity they are. Thus Judaism will share
many beliefs with Christianity, whereas Taoism may have some
analogous beliefs about a spiritual dimension of reality in relation to which there is an appropriate way of living, but is rather
remotely like the Christian faith. There are degrees of truth in
religion – that is, some propositional beliefs are more adequately
true than others. It is unlikely that one religion has nothing but
totally true propositions, and all the other religions have nothing
but false propositions. Most religions will share some truths, and
maybe Christianity, Christians think, has the most, or the most
important, set of true propositions.

This will still seem to many to be an unjustified assertion of the
superior truth of Christianity, but why should Barth not say something like it, and avoid contradiction? It seems to be because of
his more basic belief that there is a 'divine judgment of everything
human' (71). 'In relation to God our every act is in vain, even in
the best life' (73). This is certainly a belief some Christians have.
But it is so widely disputed among Christians that it is odd to use
it as a basic Christian revelation. It is much more like a very pessimistic interpretation of some parts of Scripture, and as such it
seems to confirm how difficult it is to be sure what God is revealing, even if one takes Scripture very seriously. For many people

the condemnation of even the most heroic human goodness seems impossibly counter-intuitive. When I read that 'Precisely in the best that they have done they have acted sinfully towards God' (78), I feel that morality itself is being undermined, and that a God who thinks like that is rather a moral monstrosity.

My own church, the Church of England, says in the 13th article of the 39 Articles, 'Of works done before the grace of Christ … we doubt not but they have the nature of sin.' This is an article which I can only accept in a very special sense. That is, I can say that without God's forgiveness and mercy, even all the good works I do cannot deliver me from the estrangement from God which is part of unredeemed human nature. That is not because I do lots of apparent good but God regards it all as evil. It means that I fail so often in my attempts to do good that I need some help to bridge the 'moral gap' between intention and achievement.[2] It is because I cannot do what I know to be good that a reliance on good works cannot deliver me from evil. I can believe that. What I cannot bring myself to believe is that if I perform an act of heroic charity, that is sinful.

On the contrary, I believe, with St Peter, that 'in every nation anyone who fears him [God] and does what is right is acceptable to him'.[3] This did not prevent Peter from preaching the forgiveness of sins through trust in Jesus Christ. But it does imply that those who trust in God and try to do what is right, even if they have not heard of Jesus, are acceptable to God. They may be acceptable only because Jesus has died and was raised for them, and because they will be included in Christ when they come to know the truth. Nevertheless, even though good works alone will not unite them to God, good works are really good and pleasing in the sight of God.

---

[2] See John Hare, *The Moral Gap* (Oxford: Clarendon Press, 1996) for an excellent discussion of this topic.

[3] Acts 10, 35.

Good Works and Faith

Although Barth is very scathing about good works, he actually recognises that they are necessary to salvation, which is fellowship
with God. Faith, he says, is not only trust in God's promises. It is
also commitment to love and to obey God. A person of faith cannot say, 'I love God, but I will continue to be proud and hateful.'
The devils who 'believe and tremble'[4] presumably believe that God
exists, but do not have faith. So, though Christians sometimes say,
'God forgives unconditionally', they do not really mean that. God
stands *ready* to forgive anyone, but the condition of forgiveness is
repentance and the resolution to obey God.

Barth devotes some time to explaining that the Torah, the Jewish
law, was a matter of grace and not of works, even though it gives
very detailed accounts of the good works that are required of believers. It is almost impossible to see how he can say this, if he thinks
that even good works are sinful. It requires what he might call a
'Jesuitical' frame of mind to say that good works are sinful, but God
requires them of believers.

If there is a 'law of love', then some acts are right and others are
wrong. The New Testament letters contain lists of things that are
wrong and things that are right, sometimes insisting that those
who do wrong are to be excluded from the community unless they
repent.[5] But if there are things that are right, that God requires, then
those things logically cannot be sins, things that God prohibits.
Therefore there is right and wrong, good and evil, whether people
have faith in God or not.

The Bible itself says that God is love, and that 'everyone who
loves is born of God and knows God'.[6] It is hard to square this
with Barth's insistence that even our best acts are sinful. It clearly

---

[4] James 2, 19.
[5] 1 Corinthians 5, 13: 'Drive out the wicked person from among you.'
[6] 1 John 4, 7.

entails that those who love already in some sense know God. I think we might say that they know a very important part of what God is, even if they do not consciously believe in God. That is because they tacitly believe there are objective moral demands, which are in fact rooted in the mind of God. However, it is true that doing good is not the same as, and does not depend on, trusting in God. Some of the most morally heroic people in history did not believe in God. They did not have any conscious relationship with or encounter with God, and often did not believe that the universe itself is the good creation of God, in which love would ultimately triumph.

Barth's acceptance that Judaism before Jesus is a form of divine revelation, in which God is truly known, shows that there can be genuine revelation where Jesus is not known. The Protestant rejection of 'good works' can be seen as a way of saying that one cannot achieve fellowship with God just by performing ritual acts like sacrifices, penances, and pilgrimages. This was a position already taken by many Hebrew prophets.[7] It does not mean that such things should not be done. It means that love and justice are necessary parts of true worship, and if they are lacking all religious rituals are indeed vain. But it should be obvious that many religions insist on the renunciation of self and the love of others as necessary parts of true worship. It is not that good acts are vain or even sinful. That is false, and it is an extremely dangerous teaching, in a world in which so many people have no religious faith. Commitment to good is absolutely necessary for all without exception. What belief in God adds is that there is the hope that goodness will triumph, that our moral failures will be forgiven, that there will be a personal fulfilment of life that is possible for all, and that there is a mind of perfect goodness who will support our efforts to act justly and compassionately. That is salvation, the fulfilment of life in happiness and

---

[7] Isaiah 1, 14: 'Your new moons and your appointed festivals my soul hates', and Isaiah 1, 17: 'Learn to do good, seek justice, rescue the oppressed.'

goodness. Efforts to be good will lead us towards such a life. The Christian teaching is that, though we fail to achieve goodness in so many ways, there is a spiritual power which will forgive our failures, make us truly capable of love, liberate us from our sufferings, and bring all to share in perfect goodness. Of course this will involve our assent and co-operation, our trust, our faith, and our hope.

This means that one should be sceptical about Barth's claim that our forgiveness and sanctification (being made actually loving and good) are without reference to any merit or activities of our own. It is true that Jews are not chosen to be Jews because they are better or wiser than other people. Christians are not chosen to be Christians because they are more loving or intelligent than others. But Jews rarely think, as some deluded Christians do, that they have been chosen to be given eternal life, while others are destined for Hell. They are chosen to proclaim to the world the love and forgiveness and empowerment of God.[8] Election by God is the calling to obey, not to rule. That call to obedience does lay particular demands on people. Christians may not be chosen for their intelligence, but they are chosen to strive for love and goodness. So it can be misleading to say, as Barth does, that 'God has reconciled Godless man.' This gives the paradoxical impression – and Barth can never resist a paradox – that Christians are both condemned and forgiven at the same time. The image is that of the 'justified sinner', one who remains a sinner and yet is treated as sinless by God.

That image is not wrong, but it is misleading if it is thought to imply that one can continue sinning and yet be seen as sinless by God. The one who is justified (forgiven) is one who is repentant and committed to works of love. She may fail, she will fail, to love fully and truly, but if she relies on the help of God to be transfigured by the love of God, her failures will be forgiven. It is therefore better to speak, not just of justified sinners, but of penitent and God-seeking

---

[8] Exodus 19, 6: 'You shall be for me a priestly kingdom and a holy nation.'

forgiven sinners. Such a one is not chosen by God to be forgiven for no particular reason. All, not just some, are challenged to repent, and it is those who respond who are forgiven for their penitence and obedient trust in a God who can in time bring them to share in perfect goodness. Justification is neither the imputation of goodness where it does not actually exist (for God does not lie), nor the instantaneous making just of those who repent (for humans continue to fail). Justification is the beginning of a process in which love of self is slowly overcome by divine help to make one able to share in the divine nature.

Predestination and Compatibilism

Barth seeks to deny that humans play an active, causal part in redemption, something additional to the initial act of God's providence, which is necessary for salvation. It may seem that humans must actively repent and profess faith before they can be redeemed.[9] This may be taken to show that God does not wholly and unilaterally determine their actions. But Barth insists that total divine determination and free human action are compatible.

It must be allowed that this is a traditional Christian view. It follows from a conception of God as simple, timeless, and impassible. God is simple, and cannot possess complex properties.[10] Time, having many parts, is complex, and so God cannot have any properties that are temporal. God is timeless, and so cannot change in any respect, because time is the measure of change, and without time there can be no change. God is impassible, and so cannot be changed by anything that happens in time.

---

[9] 'Our Heavenly Father … hath promised forgiveness of sins to all them that with hearty repentance and true faith turn unto him', from the Anglican 1662 Prayer Book Absolution.

[10] Aquinas, Summa Theologiae, 1a 2, question 3.

I do not think any of these properties are mentioned in the Bible, though the thought that God is the creator of time and space may be taken to imply that God is not in time, or is not in our space-time, anyway. The idea is really a philosophical one, which derives from Plato and Aristotle.

There are some Biblical views which support the idea. Prophecy is best accounted for if the future is foreknown by God. Biblical prophecies, however, are usually framed in rather general and ambiguous terms. They could be speaking of future events that God had determined to happen in a rather general way, but not in all their particular details. It is quite possible to think that God determines and foreknows the future in a general way (for instance, that there will be people who form a community of the Spirit, or that many or all people will have eternal life), while leaving open many specific acts to the determination of finite personal beings.

An often quoted Biblical passage in support of predestination is Paul's letter to the Romans, which states that 'those whom he [God] foreknew he also predestined ... and those whom he predestined he also called, and those whom he called he also justified, and those whom he justified he also glorified'.[11] This does seem to state that God foreknew and predestined some specific people to be glorified, though it does not say that many, or even all, others were not going to be glorified. Paul's thought is difficult and sometimes paradoxical. This passage could be taken as saying that God knew and predestined that (made sure that) there would be some people (not specifically identified) whom God called, justified, and glorified, as members of the body of Christ. That leaves it open what happens to those who will not be called to that specific vocation.

However, predestination became a central belief for Calvinists. God creates the whole of time, from beginning to end, in one non-temporal act. If this is so, God knows exactly what has happened, what is happening, and what will happen, in time. This is not

---

[11] Romans 8, 29–30.

quite foreknowledge, which implies that God knows things before (i.e. at a time) before they happen. It is rather eternal, timeless, and changeless knowledge.

One traditional view (Molinism)[12] holds that God eternally knows all times, and determines all things in one non-temporal creative act, but that does not entail that created beings do not make free decisions. I have never been convinced by this argument. It accepts that God must, in the very same act, create every event in time. So when a person decides something, God not only knows what she will decide, but God has already, in the timeless act of creation, created the outcome of that decision. Therefore the person can only decide the future that God timelessly creates.

Nonetheless, we can certainly say, according to compatibilists, that this is a free decision. Namely, it is not compelled by any other person, and it is the result of a conscious choice. This choice has to be what God has eternally decreed. It could not be otherwise, except in the sense that there is a logical possibility (an alternative choice is stateable without contradiction), but not a real possibility, that the choice could have been made differently.

This can be put by saying that what God eternally knows is what God eternally decrees. Absolute omniscience, which includes knowledge of every time from the first to the last moment, entails absolute predestination; otherwise there is no way of guaranteeing that God knows absolutely everything. If such a compatibilist view is correct, I think, as Schleiermacher did, that universal salvation is the only acceptable option for a Christian, since it is easy for God to determine all creatures to salvation if God is wholly determining their actions and if God is omnipotent and wholly good.[13]

---

[12] Luis de Molina was a sixteenth-century Jesuit, whose view is still held by some scholars today, Alvin Plantinga being one.

[13] 'Mercy ... is incompatible with the permanent exclusion of some from the communicated blessedness of Christ': Schleiermacher, *The Christian Faith*, p. 544 (para. 118).

Divine and Human Freedom

Barth seems to accept a compatibilist theory. For instance, Barth holds that God made a free personal decision to create the universe, though it could hardly be said that the Bible ever explicitly states that. The Bible certainly states that God created the world, but it makes no remark about whether this was necessary or free, whether God created other worlds, or whether this was the best of all possible worlds. Barth says, 'In Him [Christ] the created world is already perfect in spite of its imperfection ... it will be seen to be the best of all possible worlds.'[14] This last phrase is one of the most famous, and most contentious, metaphysical doctrines of Leibniz, which is nowhere to be found in the Bible or any Christian credal document. It was lampooned by Voltaire in his novel *Candide*. For many people, the existence of suffering undermines any suggestion that there could be no better world than this, and to say that something is perfect 'in spite of its imperfection' is like saying that something is round in spite of its squareness. It does not make sense. It also seems obvious that there are many incommensurable kinds of goodness, so there is no world that is better in every respect than any other possible world.[15] In any case, this is a prime piece of metaphysics, whether it makes sense or not.

I do not think we can hope to know whether God was free to create or not. There is something odd in talking of a free eternal decision, if only because eternity seems to imply changelessness, and free decisions seem to imply the possibility of change.

However, when Barth speaks of 'freedom', he offers a highly metaphysical, and highly provocative, analysis. He holds that 'human freedom ... does not allow for any vague choices between various possibilities'.[16] Again, 'human freedom is the God-given freedom

---

[14] Barth, *Church Dogmatics*, volume III, part 1, p. 385.
[15] Aquinas makes this point in *Summa Theologiae*, 6, question 25, p. 175.
[16] 'The Gift of Freedom', in Barth, *The Humanity of God*, p. 77.

to obey'.[17] This is not the freedom to disobey God; 'The idea that man can conquer freedom as God's antagonist ... is untenable.'[18] He does not see freedom as the ability to obey or disobey God. Since God commands obedience to the moral law, it follows that human freedom is not the freedom to choose to do right or wrong.

Human acts, for good or ill, are determined by God. This idea certainly finds a place in the Bible. But so does the belief that humans are responsible for choosing between good and evil, and will be rewarded or punished accordingly, which resounds throughout the Old Testament.[19] It is very difficult, perhaps impossible, to decide which view is 'Biblical'.

My own view is that divine punishment is only acceptable if humans are free to become God's antagonists, and that they have in fact done so. Barth strongly emphasises God's judgment on sin, but also holds that God predestines all human actions. This makes it extremely difficult to account for sin and evil in creation, a difficulty – Barth might say 'a mystery' – which seems to me a major stumbling-block to faith.

If this is Barth's account of freedom, it seems that when he says God freely determines God's own actions, he does not mean that God had a choice between various possibilities. A God who had such a choice would, he says, 'be a demon'.[20] 'God's own freedom is Trinitarian', he says, which I think means that it is grounded in God's nature as love. God's freedom is simply God's acting in accordance with the divine nature, not being determined by another. In other words, God's freedom is identical with God's necessity, not as a metaphysical principle, but as a personal act.

This distinction between a metaphysical principle and a personal act is, it seems to me, a distinction without a difference. Such

[17] Ibid., p. 82.
[18] Ibid., p. 76.
[19] See Deuteronomy 30, 19: 'I have set before you life and death, blessings and curses. Choose life.'
[20] 'The Gift of Freedom', in Barth, *The Humanity of God*, p. 71.

a personal act is a metaphysical principle, because it asserts that the ultimate reality (the prime subject of metaphysics) is in some sense personal. God's act of creation, according to Barth, is not an external and constrained one, but something essential to the divine nature, to which there is no real alternative. That is quite a widely held view, but it is certainly a metaphysical view. The view is perhaps implied in parts of the Bible, but denied in other parts. So here a metaphysical preference is influencing the interpretation of Scripture, and influencing what is taken to be revelation.

Similarly, Barth's claim that creation is free, that God had no need to create, and could be loving without creation (which seems to conflict with the compatibilist assertion that God's freedom is not a choice between alternatives) is not stated anywhere in the Bible. This again is a speculation about the divine aseity, which is thought by some philosophers to entail that God is in need of nothing. There are many, including me, who think that God could not be agapic, self-giving, love without creating genuine others (not just other 'persons' within God, who would be incapable of sin) to love. Whatever one thinks, this also is genuine philosophical speculation. As the philosopher Hegel said, the issue is not whether to have a metaphysics or not, it is what sort of metaphysics you have. The Bible's metaphysics may be rather varied and rather hard to pin down, but it is there at its very heart.

Three Incoherences

Barth's view of freedom entails that all human acts are predetermined, or eternally determined, by God. Yet he believes that all human acts are also faithless and are 'enemies of grace'. I think that this view is incoherent in three ways.

It is incoherent to say that a loving God determines what every person will do, and then say that all of them, even the best and most morally heroic of human acts, are condemned by the God who created them. It is incoherent to say that all religions are faithless, and then say that one of them is actually given directly by God. And it is incoherent to say that a religion of law and ritual practice (ancient Judaism) is a means of grace and forgiveness, and then say that only in the name of Jesus Christ can divine grace and forgiveness be found.

These incoherencies all arise from setting up two mutually exclusive alternative beliefs which are both said to be true at the same time. The actual human situation is that humans are faced with complex sets of choices, when often there is much to be said both for and against most of them. Thus we do not have to say that all religions are totally faithless, and that some alleged divine revelation is totally true. We do not have to say that good works are sinful, and that God commands them. And we do not have to say that only in the name of Jesus Christ can divine forgiveness and grace be found, and that it can also be found in a Judaism which did not yet know about Jesus.

One can say positively that moral laws are ordained by God, but that trust in divine grace may be needed to forgive our failure always to obey such laws. We can say that some religious attitudes (the practice of ritual without the practice of justice) are faithless, but many (praying humbly to God) are not. We can say that even religions which are believed to be divinely revealed may contain human inadequacies and errors, and the existence of such errors does not necessarily condemn a religion. And we can believe that Jesus is the one through whom divine forgiveness is mediated to the world, but it is not necessary that all should be explicitly aware of this in order to be forgiven.

The Futility of Seeking God

Barth rejects all such attempts to avoid incoherence by insisting that there can be no mixture of divine initiation and human reception in the notion of religion. 'Man's attempts to know God … are futile – wholly and completely'(72). For Barth, God is known only in Jesus Christ. All human images and ideas of God are arbitrary and wilful products of the imagination. Unless God speaks to us, revealing Godself, we cannot gain a true view of God. The attempt to form notions of or prove the existence of God by human reason alone is doomed to failure. Revelation is required if we are to have any genuine knowledge of God.

Many world religions would agree with Barth that revelation is necessary to true religion, and that reason alone cannot give an adequate idea of God. At some point, the gods of many religions appear in visions and dreams, and speak through holy people, prophets, or oracles. Prophets and seers do not think that they are making up or inventing their ideas of God. They usually claim that the gods appear to them and speak to them. In early Hebrew religion, God appears to Abraham and speaks to him.[21] In other ancient religions much the same thing is said to happen. This is not a matter of religions without revelation. It is a claim that visions of the gods appear to holy persons. If these visions conflict in what they say, they cannot all be truthful. But how is one to tell which are truthful and which are not? Barth assumes that only the Christian one is truthful. Yet devout Muslims say the same thing about the God of Islam. It is hard to see how one could decide which is truthful without some attempt to see if there are alleged facts or injunctions in the revelation which are known on independent grounds to be untrue or immoral. This means that revelations are subject to rational inspection and to judgment of their content. They cannot therefore be unshakeable and certain standards of truth which are not subject to factual or ethical criticism.

It is odd to say that all religions except Christianity are futile constructs of the imagination, when they often claim to record revelatory encounters with spiritual powers. Even in Judaism and Islam, which forbid visual images of God, there are many verbal

---

[21] Genesis 12, 1.

descriptions of God as sitting on a throne or as speaking to prophets and patriarchs.[22] At least in the case of Judaism, Barth allows that such verbal images of God are legitimate revelations of God. He has to do so, since the Old Testament records of them are parts of Christian Scripture too. Therefore there is one non-Christian religion which at least used to have genuine revelations of God. So it is false that all man's attempts to know God are futile. Christians and Jews do know the true God, and if them, why not many other religions which claim to be founded on revelation also?

The obvious reason is that alleged revelations contradict each other, so they cannot all be true. That is correct. But it does not mean that everything about human religions is false. One obvious possibility is that religions are mixtures of truth and falsity, of human imaginary constructions and divine revelations. That is a very different picture from the one Barth paints. But it is perhaps more charitable to many religions, less triumphalist about Christianity, and more consistent with an idea of God as concerned with all humanity, not condemning all religions except one, which God chooses freely, that is to say not on merit or expertise.

---

[22] Isaiah 40, 22: 'It is he who sits above the circle of the earth.'

7 | The Failure of Philosophy

God and Philosophy

Barth admits that ideas of God exist in many religions, and this points to a longing for meaning and hope in existence which is almost universal in human societies. However, there is an almost infinite variety of ideas of God. They often contradict one another. They seem to show a great skill in the invention of various images of God or the gods, but these seem to be precisely inventions rather than to be accurate representations of God. They are often mingled with elements of waywardness and violence. And their great diversity gives rise to some uncertainty about the truth of any of them.

All these things are true. The problem is why Barth should seek to exempt the Christian idea of God from these facts. There is no one Christian idea of God. There is the quasi-Aristotelian idea of God as timeless, passionless, and changeless, firmly rooted in Catholic tradition. There is the panentheistic idea of God as including the universe of time and change. There is the Process theology idea of God as suffering and as patiently influencing the universe by love. There is the Idealist idea of God as a cosmic mind or person. There is the idea of God as a Trinity of three conscious persons. There is the idea of God the Trinity as strictly one mind and will, but with three aspects. And there are others. Variety of ideas of God is not merely between different religions. It exists within the Christian religion too. So variety and diversity are not objections to revelation. They are indicators that alleged revelations are subject to factual and ethical assessment.

If it is said that religious visions are all products of human imagination, this is in a sense true. Humans imagine that they are encountered by spiritual powers outside themselves, and as they think about these encounters, they often design images which represent them. It is just the same in Christianity. Throughout the ages, many Christians have claimed that Jesus has appeared to them. Though no one actually knows what Jesus looked like, many images of Jesus have been constructed by Christian imaginations. Those images can vary quite widely, often reflecting the culture of the societies in which they are produced, though some images have become standard. Anyone who knows Palestine will be very sceptical about the blue-eyed, fair-haired images of Jesus that are standard in Europe and the USA. Human imagination does play a large part in many religions, but that is quite compatible with believing that such images are representations of a real existent spiritual reality.

If it is said that some ideas of God are wayward and violent, then one has to admit that some Christian ideas seem wayward and violent too – the idea that God chooses some to be saved, regardless of merit, can seem wayward; and the idea that God calls for the destruction of infidels and heretics is violent.

It is also very difficult to be really certain which of these ideas is correct. Looked at from outside, they make very similar claims, and that must decrease the certainty with which one adheres solely to one of them.

So Christian ideas of God are in much the same boat as many other ideas of God. Indeed, the God of Judaism, Islam, and Sikhism is described in ways exactly like some descriptions of the Christian God. If two descriptions of God, whether in the same or in different religions, are identical, then they are speaking of gods which are alike, not wholly different. All the Abrahamic religions describe God as the powerful and wise creator of the world, and they are thus speaking of Gods who are in many respects similar, or if the descriptions are virtually identical, then they are speaking of the same God, even if they go on to give different additional descriptions of God.

Yet Barth insists that 'God is not to be found in the series of gods.'[1] God is 'wholly Other' (*Ganz Andere*, a phrase taken from Rudolf Otto, which looks suspiciously philosophical), and not at all speculative. As far as descriptions go, this is simply false. All the Christian ideas of God just mentioned are speculative to some extent.

Barth says that God is never sought, nor discovered, and that God does not correspond to a human disposition or possibility in any way. It is hard to make sense of this. If humans can ever encounter God, it must be possible for them to do so, and that is a human possibility. Did St Augustine not seek and long for God? And did he not discover God after giving up Manichean ideas? The Psalms speak of longing for God: 'As a deer longs for the running brooks, so longs my soul for you, O God.'[2] God fulfils every longing in the human soul. The Bible speaks of longing for and of discovering God. It also speaks positively of seeking God – 'Seek the Lord while he may be found.'[3]

If we can seek and long for God, we must have some idea of what we are seeking. If God was totally unlike anything we expect or think of, how could we seek God? If God was really 'wholly Other', how could we identify God as creator of worlds? God could of course say, 'I am the creator of worlds.' But if God spoke, God would not be wholly Other. God would be capable of speech, and thus be known as something like a personal intelligent agent. That might not be all God was, but God would be at least capable of truly appearing to us as a personal agent.

I can only conclude that God can be sought and longed for, and is capable of appearing to us as personal. Thus God is not totally unknowable or wholly Other.

---

[1] Karl Barth, *Dogmatics in Outline* (London: SCM Press, 1949), p. 36.
[2] Psalm 42, 1.
[3] Isaiah 55, 6.

Natural Theology and Metaphysics

What Barth is most famously known for is his opposition to natural theology and to metaphysics, to any possibility of knowing God without revelation, and, he thinks, specifically the revelation in Jesus Christ.

The word 'metaphysics' has a varied set of meanings, but one main meaning is that it is the study of what sorts of beings exist (ontology), and what their characteristics and relationships to each other are.

I think that what Barth has in mind when he uses the term is Hegel's philosophy of Absolute Idealism. Hegel has been interpreted as saying that religion is a picturesque and metaphorical description of reality, which is capable of approaching the metaphysical truth that *Geist* or Spirit is the ultimate reality which unfolds its nature progressively in time. Interpreted in this way, religion would be subordinate to philosophy.

In opposition to this view, Barth wished to assert the primacy of divine revelation, and held that human reason alone could not reliably arrive at knowledge of God – there is 'no universal deity capable of being reached conceptually'.[4] But of course this itself is a metaphysical statement. It says that there is a God who reveals the divine nature to created humans in a particular way – through Jesus Christ. And it adds that humans are incapable of describing God accurately without the help of revelation.

One problem is that if there is no way of describing God accurately, no one could ever be sure that it was God who was alleged to be revealing something. Jesus could, after all, have been a mistaken prophet (as Jews generally think he was), or people might mistake their own ideas for revelations from a superior being (they often do so, apparently). One needs to have some reasons for thinking there is a creator God if belief in divine revelation is to be credible. The provision of such reasons would be part of metaphysics.

[4] Barth, *The Humanity of God*, p. 48.

Even if a revelation is accepted as genuine, it still needs to be interpreted. A revelation in and through Jesus is particularly complex. One will need to say what gives a human person such authority, whether it is his words or his acts that matter most, whether his words and acts have been reliably recorded, and how they are to be applied in the very different conditions of human lives thousands of years later. Of course this can be done, and Barth wrote thousands of words in doing it. The point is that Barth's interpretations are at least partly new and original, products of his own thinking and not just relays of direct messages from God, or repetitions of what the Bible says.

An illustration of this point is that, when speaking of revelation, Barth writes, 'To say revelation is to say "the Word became flesh".'[5] This is already to show a preference for John's Gospel over the three synoptic Gospels. John shows a preference for cosmic speculations about divine–human unity over more straightforward historical narratives. It should be clear that a great deal of metaphysical explanation is needed to expound what is meant by 'the Word', and how it could become 'flesh'. This would be properly metaphysical, because it would have to say what sort of existent the Word was, and how it related to the space-time world. That is the sort of thing that metaphysics (at least as I have taught it for many years) does, even or especially if some of its basic data come from revelation. Perhaps if Barth had been more familiar with the Indian traditions of metaphysical thought, in Vedanta for instance, which takes revelation as its starting point, he would have seen that metaphysics and faith are not at all to be opposed, but often relate very closely to each other.

Knowing God

A revelation involves an apprehension of spiritual reality. Though Barth claims that revelations do not depend on prior philosophical

[5] Barth, *Church Dogmatics*, volume I, part 1, p. 109.

presuppositions, apprehensions of a spiritual reality do not generally come as complete surprises to people who have no philosophical background which influences their interpretation of such apprehensions. They come to prophets and sages in various ways, as apprehensions of an objective moral law, or of a supremely desirable being to whom devotion is appropriate, or of a sense of union with the underlying reality of all things, or of a reality which cannot be adequately described, but which delivers one from suffering and the anxiety of being.

These might all be seen as aspects of spiritual reality, which the teachers of the great spiritual traditions of the world claim to have experienced in a unique and overwhelming way. The idea of a personal creator God is just one way of describing spiritual reality, which is prevalent in the Abrahamic tradition. It can hardly be described as futile, since it involves a philosophical exploration of ways of describing the spiritual dimension, which according to Christians turns out to be roughly right – God is a personal spiritual creator. While there may be no knock-down proof that there is such a God, the idea of it may be elaborated conceptually. Indeed, it would need to be, if an interpretation of spiritual apprehension as experience of God is ever to be taken as correct.

Barth's attitude to the futility of philosophy changed somewhat over the years. In a short talk given in 1953[6] he says, 'A free theologian does not deny, nor is he ashamed of, his indebtedness to a particular philosophy or ontology.' This seems to imply that philosophy, even metaphysics, may form a background to theological thought. However, he also says that 'His ontology will be subject to criticism and control by his theology.' Biblical truth must take the leading and controlling role, and so adherence to revelation must precede philosophical speculation. Yet that is an admission that some type of metaphysics may be especially helpful in shaping theological thinking.

[6] Barth, 'The Gift of Freedom', in *The Humanity of God*, p. 92.

The relation of philosophical thought and revelation may be even closer, because some initial philosophical commitment (one that admits the possibility of a superior spiritual, conscious, reality) is necessary before claims that Jesus mediates such a reality can gain any purchase. Then, in deciding what interpretation to take of the very diverse writings that comprise the Bible, some philosophical views (perhaps a reformative view of punishment, or a moral assessment of what divine perfection requires) may play an important part. As a matter of fact, in Barth's case, both these factors seem to be present. For that reason, Barth undermines his own stark opposition to metaphysical thinking, yet without producing a fully coherent alternative.

If we examine the Biblical record, we can trace a historical development in the idea of God. Beginning with polytheistic ideas, with the 'God of Abraham' being one god among many,[7] the major prophets concluded that there was only one creator God.[8] That could hardly have been derived just from the apprehension itself, since any alleged revelation such as 'I am the only Lord' could well have been illusory. Its acceptance as genuine depends upon a process of reflection about the dependence of all things on God. That, if not natural theology, is certainly rational reflection, which is needed to get an acceptable interpretation of revelatory experiences.

The process of development also involves moral reflection. The idea of a wrathful God who commanded the extermination of Canaanites, or who killed people for touching the sacred Ark, even by accident, was sublimated by the idea of a God of love who desired even the love of enemies. For Christians, this process reached an apex in Jesus, who taught that there was an afterlife when God desired all people to live in God forever.

This process of reflection continues as we learn more about the size and age of the cosmos, and the process of evolution. Revelation,

---

[7] Exodus 18, 11: 'the Lord is greater than all gods'.
[8] Isaiah 45, 5: 'I am the Lord and there is no other; besides me there is no god.'

in the form of apprehensions of God by prophets and seers, is continually being reinterpreted in the light of new factual and moral developments, from both within and without the Christian faith.

This account is very different from Barth's picture of knowledge of a being which is totally different from any human desire or inclination, requires no philosophical or independent confirmation, and comes to people who are not expecting or hoping for it. Yet Jesus seems to fit, even if he also surpassed and fulfilled, the pattern of the patriarchs and prophets of Israel, who apprehended Spirit as a personal God who made moral demands, whose perfect love inspired devotion, who was the one source of all things, and who delivers humanity from the slavery of desire. Jesus truly sublimates the teaching of those who went before him. It could also be said that, when seen in this way, he sublimates the teachings of many religious traditions, which grasp part, but truly grasp, what God is.

The Revelation of God in Christ

Most Christians would want to say that Jesus had a unique insight into the mind of God, and that God acted in and through him in a unique way to show the divine nature and purpose. They would agree with Barth that 'God makes himself knowable to man' through Jesus.[9] But this does not entail that God has not made himself known to humans in other ways. And it does not entail that 'God is he who is to be found in the books of the Old and New Testaments',[10] if what is meant is that everything said about God in the Bible is true.

God is made known at least to Jews, Muslims, and Sikhs, who all believe in a personal creator God. I see little difficulty in saying that something of God is made known to those who accept an objective

---

[9] Barth, *Dogmatics in Outline*, p. 37.
[10] Ibid.

moral law, a higher spiritual reality, and a way of liberation from suffering and evil. I see nothing wrong with saying that God has 'disclosed himself' in the Bible, or in Jesus, though one needs to be aware of the violent and vengeful views of God which are sometimes found there, but which were sublimated by Jesus.

I see no reason to say that only the Bible shows what God is, when many other Scriptures agree with much of what the Bible says. Barth later explicitly stated as much,[11] so his statements about knowledge of God being impossible without Christian revelation should probably be seen as exaggerated and rhetorical. It seems that what he really meant was that non-Biblical views of God, insofar as they are true, are in fact products of inspiration by the Biblical God in a partly hidden way. Further, all non-Biblical views are mixed with error and uncertainty, so they are at best partial and imperfect ideas of God. The truth they possess is in fact due to the Spirit of God, and depends totally on the one fully true revelation in Jesus Christ, and can only be correctly seen for what it is from the perspective of faith in Christ.

When Barth comes to say what the revealed nature of God is, he writes that God is 'a living, acting, working Subject',[12] a personal agent who creates the universe out of desire for an 'other', not because God needs any other, but because God freely chooses to do so, out of love. Further, God acts in history, and Barth insists that the Bible is a history book, not a philosophical tract, which records God's acts, and in that way, not by speculation, shows what God is.

My reservation here is that, though the Bible is largely about the history of Israel, and about God's active relation to Israel, it is not devoid of speculation. The history of Israel is interpreted in terms of the severe demands of the Torah, judgment on Israel for her failure to obey the Torah, the possibility of forgiveness for those who repent and obey God, the promise of empowerment by God's

---

[11] In Barth, *Church Dogmatics*, volume IV, part 3.
[12] Barth, *Dogmatics in Outline*, p. 38.

Spirit, and the promise of peace and prosperity in some earthly future. These are not straightforward historical beliefs. They are about seeing historical events in relation to a spiritual reality which demands, judges, forgives, empowers, and promises, who is in other words truly personal. One of the strong points of Barth's theology is that the personal action of God in history, who in Jesus unites human and divine natures, and thus includes humans as participants in a dynamic and interactive history with God, takes centre stage.

When speaking of God's revelation in Jesus Christ, Barth's interpretation of Jesus Christ is nevertheless very speculative, untraditional, and philosophically influenced. It is opposed to most of earlier Christian thinking. It was central to Barth's thinking to hold that Jesus took upon himself the condemnation due to man because of sin, 'in order that it [sin] may no longer affect us and that we may no longer place ourselves under it. What takes place in God's humanity is ... the *affirmation* of man' (emphasis in the original).[13]

When one examines this statement closely, it reveals itself to be very unusual. What is odd is that the union of divine and human natures in Christ is such that it includes human nature – that is, the nature of every human – in the condemnation that sin deserves, and that Jesus has taken on himself. But it also includes human nature – and thus every individual human being – in the resurrected life of union and fellowship with God. Because the condemnation has been taken by Christ in the crucifixion, it could be said that it no longer applies to us. But the resurrection of Jesus to eternal fellowship with God does apply to us, and so all of humanity is reconciled to God. This difference between the condemnation that no longer applies and the reconciliation that does apply underlies Barth's paradoxical thesis that humans are both 'monsters' and 'affirmed by God' at the same time.

---

[13] Barth, *The Humanity of God*, p. 60.

A New Testament phrase which at first sight seems to support Barth's interpretation is: 'as all die in Adam, so all will be made alive in Christ'.[14] That implies that the sufferings humans endure are the results of human estrangement from God. Jesus shares in that suffering, and so in him the divine shares in human suffering and in the consequences of human sin. Then the resurrection of Jesus shows that humanity is assumed into the divine life. It is not the case that, as in many accounts of the Atonement, Jesus takes a punishment which humans deserve, and therefore humans are (rather unfairly, it may seem) released from that punishment. That is a juridical view of the Atonement, which sees God demanding the payment of a penalty, but then, rather oddly, God paying it in person. But Barth begins to move away from this traditional approach to atonement, and adopts a more participative view.

The participative view is that in Jesus Christ, humanity and divinity are united. When Barth uses the name 'Jesus Christ', he means by that not just the historical Jesus of Nazareth, but the eternal Word of God, in which humanity now shares. As Barth puts it, 'sharing in the life of the Son of God ... is precisely the name Jesus Christ' (147). Because human and divine natures are united in Christ, the divine nature in Christ participates in human suffering. This is indeed 'a death for us', but it is not the payment of a penalty. It is the decision of God to share in the estrangement of the human condition.

This stress on God, even in the divine nature, sharing in human suffering, is a marked change from the traditional view that, while God suffers in the human nature of Jesus, the divine nature, being perfect, remains untouched by suffering. This is one point at which Barth's interpretation of the passion of Christ is both innovative and not immediately derivable from Scripture itself. A more crucial creative move is found in the interpretation of Christ's resurrection as the inclusion of human nature – every individual human – in

[14] 1 Corinthians 15, 22.

the life of God. Thereby humanity is affirmed. The promise is that all humans can, or perhaps even already do, share in the divine life.

Barth has not consistently freed himself from some Reformation ideas that Jesus' death pays the penalty of sin, that humanity is totally depraved, and that salvation is the unmerited salvation of a predestined elect. Even in his later writings, he does not escape such ideas, which partly accounts for his ambiguities about the need for metaphysical thought, the possibility of revelation in the non-Christian world, and the prospect of universal salvation.

But he begins to transform those doctrines into a rather different picture of the divine Christ sharing in human suffering, to give assurance that suffering human nature can, in every human life, be united to and affirmed by God.

It is this insistence that the eternal Christ participates in the human condition and enables humanity to participate in the divine life that distinguished Barth's theology from that of Harnack, who regarded such doctrines as obsolete myths. Harnack regarded talk of an eternal Word uniting human nature to itself as too metaphysical. This is ironic, for metaphysics is precisely what Barth wanted to disentangle from faith.

It is not the case, however, as Barth says, that after the death of Christ sin no longer affects us or that we need not regard ourselves as any longer under its power. It seems obvious that even after we confess that Jesus died for us, we continue to sin and to a large extent remain under its power. As Luther said, we do not actually become perfect. We are justified sinners, still sinful and yet justified.

On a participative view of the matter, humans continue to sin, but seeing Christ's sharing in our sufferings, we may be moved to repent and turn to him in trust. Then the risen Christ will begin to empower us to 'live in him' and be gradually transformed by the power of the Spirit. The paradox disappears, because humans become, not haters of God, but people of penitent faith whom God will transform into the image of Christ. They will see in Jesus Christ the nature of God as one who has compassion on suffering, and who desires and can effect the reconciliation of all to God.

It must be said that this interpretation of what is revealed in Jesus is not unequivocally clear and agreed by all. For instance, many Jews and Christians would not regard the Biblical God as creating and sustaining the universe out of all-forgiving love. For them, God is a severe Judge, and large parts of the Old Testament threaten punishment and destruction for the sins of Israel. Only a remnant will be saved from the wrath of God, and the promise of peace is for a future time in history, when God will destroy the wicked and bring in a new Heaven and earth.[15]

It is true that Jesus takes away the judgment on humanity and replaces it with the sanctification of humanity. But when expounding this rather basic Christian doctrine, Barth relies on a selective interpretation of the Gospel records, even if one thinks it is a justifiable and illuminating one.

In the Gospels, Jesus speaks words of judgment as well as words of grace and forgiveness. There is grace, but it is not clear that it replaces judgment. For those who do not repent, judgment remains, and it often sounds final. 'The Son of Man will send his angels, and they will collect out of his kingdom all causes of sin and all evildoers, and they will throw them into the furnace of fire, where there will be weeping and gnashing of teeth.'[16]

Within Christian tradition, Greek Orthodox churches often contain an image of Christ Pantocrator, 'ruler of all', and this depicts Christ as a stern and all-powerful judge, who will separate the good from the evil before the throne of the 'last judgment'. In medieval depictions of this judgment, the damnation of sinners looks much more terrifying, and is drawn with much greater detail and creative skill than the rather boring portrayal of the salvation of the

---

[15] Nahum 1, 1–6: 'A jealous and avenging God is the Lord ... who can endure the heat of his anger?'

[16] Matthew 13, 41.

righteous and faithful. This seems very different from the Christ of Barth, who does condemn the sins of humanity, but who also takes the condemnation upon himself, thus releasing humanity from it and uniting humanity to himself in glory.

There are strands of the New Testament that imply universal salvation, and other strands that speak of 'eternal punishment'.[17] The Bible itself does not clearly and unequivocally choose between these views, and that is probably one reason why Barth does not do so either. But it means that some extra-Biblical considerations are affecting one's interpretation. These are speculative (metaphysical) speculations on how a God of love (which is affirmed clearly in the New Testament) would deal with sinners (on which there are different and opposing views in the New Testament).

Atheism and Mysticism – A Story (Very) Loosely Based on Fact

Barth spends some time in arguing that liberalism in religion has led to, and naturally or even inevitably leads to, atheism and mysticism. It is always tempting to look back at history and tell a story which shows that what happened had to happen by some sort of inner necessity. Such stories are usually very selective in the material they use, and manage to support views that are those of the storyteller. Barth's story of the progress from Reformed Christianity, through the dangers and perils of liberalism, to the emergence of atheism and mysticism, is of this type. A critical historian might be very surprised that the more usual story of progress from superstition to science has been stood on its head in this way.

Barth seems to think it was a virtue that theologians like Calvin and Luther assumed that Protestantism (in slightly different versions, of course) was the only 'true' religion, and that all other faiths were pagan aberrations. For such traditional theologians it was a disaster when scholars began to examine the Biblical

---

[17] Matthew 25, 46.

THE REVELATION OF GOD IN CHRIST

writings critically, and increased in knowledge of ancient cultures and languages. Such scholars saw problems about the reliability of Scripture, and the evidence for its total truth was seen by them to be rather scanty. Atheism became acceptable, when the hypocrisies of the Christian churches were exposed to criticism. It became apparent that absolute certainty was not appropriate for such widely disputed and unverifiable beliefs, that doctrines had changed in different cultures (the rise of Protestantism being one example of such change), and that religious beliefs were not a necessary foundation of morality.

Mysticism, by which Barth seems to mean a more apophatic view of God, had always been part of Catholic thought, but it took on new forms in German Idealism, as the traditional teachings of Christianity, with its stories of virgin births and men walking on water and being raised from the dead, came to seem less compelling to many.

But there is little reason to say that mysticism and atheism were, as Barth claims, the two major features of European thought after the Enlightenment. More important was the growth of Humanism and belief in human autonomy and creativity. There was a much greater concentration on human happiness as more important than alleged and disputed divine commands, on human equality as opposed to a divinely ordained social hierarchy, and on human rights as being universal moral norms which did not necessarily depend on religious belief. Admittedly these movements were often combined with a sense of the moral and intellectual superiority of Europeans, and a sense of mission to 'civilise' the rest of the world by colonial expansion. But such a sense of superiority and a global missionary imperative were marks of Protestant theology too.

Barth's armchair history of religion, which he claims can be corroborated in the case of all religions, a claim which any competent scholar of religion could refute, sees it as beginning with a 'formless and fruitless inner space' (whatever that may be), striving to find external form in the construction of images and laws, and then as being thrown into vacuity and uncertainty by a failure to obey the divine revelation as given in Scripture (as interpreted by Protestants).

This is ironically just the sort of highly imaginative story of the 'fall of civilisation' which fails to provide much evidence in detail for its claims that was popular with German writers of the time. I do not think it possesses much value as a historical account. Barth complains that this historical trajectory has led to religions becoming just an option (this is what he calls the non-necessity of religion), and to becoming prey to the norms and customs of constantly changing cultures (this is what he calls the weakness of religion). Barth mentions 'blood and soil', in this context, which shows that he has the descent of German culture into Nazi dictatorship in mind.

A more positive spin can be put on such a historical account. The freedom of conscience to choose or reject a religion or ideology like National Socialism is an advance on the compulsion to follow whatever faith or policy one's ruler favoured. Both have their dangers and risks, but to encourage freedom of thought is in itself a moral advance, and one that has been hard won in the modern world. One must allow, also, that the Nazis were defeated, and that in many ways a genuine concern for the welfare of all human beings has increased, at least in parts of the world. We know that this has its dangers too – Utopia is not within the grasp of humans. But it is better to promote concern for the desires and interests of all people, so far as this is possible, than to enforce obedience to some set of beliefs that someone – who, human history sadly shows, is likely to be or to turn into an unhinged dictator – thinks is good for them.

Barth argues on the strength of his allegedly historical account, that religion is 'self-contradictory'. It comes to realise that it is not necessary, but only a sort of imaginative play of pleasing or frightening images; and that it is weak, falling prey to the shifting currents of change. The result, he says, is twofold – atheism, which rejects the imagery and laws of religion, and mysticism, which gives an esoteric explanation of religion that deprives its imagery of substantial content. But, he holds, the impulse or 'religious need' continues to exist, and will generate new religions and ideologies, which will exhibit the same impulses of wilful imagination and of self-justification. I think he has in mind the ideology of National Socialism, and also Feuerbach and Hegel, the heroes or anti-heroes of atheism and mysticism, as he might put it. His conclusion is that religion is indeed a fantasy of human need and desire, and it does need to be overcome. But only 'true revelation' can overcome it, by sublimating it.

This history of the decline and fall of religion, and of its inner stronghold in 'the formless and fruitless inner space' of human need, is very much centred on the modern history of German thought. I doubt very much if a Muslim or Indian scholar could recognise it. But the chief difficulty lies in the suggestion that Evangelical Christianity could resolve the inner problems of Christianity, particularly since it has been the source of many of its problems in the Western world. The suggestion that the Evangelical movement could sublimate religion is one that has to face the problem that it too is a religion, and one that few outsiders would regard as an improvement. It has certainly led to problems, as ancient and outdated beliefs about the nature of the universe have conflicted with new scientific findings and revolutions in moral and political thought. But those problems have shown themselves to be capable of resolution.

German liberal Christianity, as in the work of Harnack for example, has seen bold experiments in rethinking Christianity to make it compatible with new knowledge, while retaining a vital spiritual core of meaning. Maybe Barth was right to protest that too much had been lost in some of these experiments, and that there was more in the ancient formulations of doctrines of Incarnation and deification than some liberal theologians allowed. But his protests are too allied to Reformation disputes which now themselves lie in the past, too tied to doctrines of election, predestination, and Biblical supremacy than much modern scholarship can accept. In particular his commitment to the Barthian Paradox that religion is faithlessness, and yet the Christian religion is true, fails to give proper recognition to the diversity and value of religious faiths, and fails to give proper attention to the shortcomings and problems of all Christian traditions, including Evangelical Protestantism.

Our global civilisation has produced in opposition to globalisation a backlash of inward-looking nationalisms which delight in opposition to those who are different, and seek power to control and oppress the lives of others. What is needed from a spiritual viewpoint is a programme that will seek the unity of humankind, the celebration of cultural diversity, and the renunciation of claims to possess the one unique truth that all should accept.

Whether the Christian set of religions can do this is moot. I think some of them can. Sadly, I do not think Karl Barth's theology can. Condemning religion, it advocates the unique truth of Christian faith, a faith which is certain, unchanging, and opposed to critical reason. It is part of the backlash against a world which has to learn to live with diversity and creative change. It looks like the dogmatics of a small and rather reactionary group of churches, not the theology of a creative movement into a more adventurous spiritual view of reality.

8 | Religion and Truth

Analysis of Barth's Third Chapter: 'The True Religion'

There are four main reasons for not using the expression 'the true religion'. One is that the word 'true' is properly applied to propositions, not to many-stranded institutions and communities of people. Saying that the Christian religion is the true religion is rather like saying that 'the English Parliament is true': it does not quite make sense.

Secondly, it gives the impression that there is only one true religion, and all the rest are false. That seems extremely short-sighted.

Thirdly, it is unclear what the true religion is. One might be tempted to say 'Christianity', but it turns out that, for Barth, it does not include most Christians – Roman Catholic and Eastern Orthodox Christians, for instance. It only seems to include members of Protestant churches who agree with Barth, and of course not all of them do. The fact that there are so many different Protestant churches should make one suspect that truth may be spread around religions, rather than being confined to a small minority, a subsection of one sort of Christians.

And fourthly, it may lead someone to think that every statement of belief that the favoured group makes is true. And there have been just too many mistakes throughout the history of religion for this to be plausible.

What Barth says is that 'we can talk about "true religion" only in the sense in which we talk about a "justified sinner"' (111). That is not very helpful. Truth and justification are not the same sorts of thing. The question of truth is the question of whether some state-ment describes some fact accurately. So a religion could be true if it describes, or rather its statements about God and the reconcili-ation of man with God describe, the facts. Any given religion may make some true statements about God, and if the statements of two different religions are more or less identical, we would have to say that these bits of different religions are both true. In this way many religions could share many true religious statements.

If a justified sinner is guilty but treated as innocent, and if a true religion is taken in an analogous sense, then a true religion would be one which is false but is treated as true. It is hard enough to explain how a guilty person could be treated as innocent, but it might be that their guilt, which is real, would not be held against them, and if repentant, they could be forgiven and helped to start again.

But it is impossible to explain how a false statement could be treated as true, although it may be possible that a person who believed a falsehood could be forgiven for their mistake and helped to find the truth. But there might be no guilt attached to anyone who believes a false statement – they might have learned it from others, and not known any better. You cannot be asked to repent of believing something false, if you had done your best to find the truth. You just have to be corrected, not forgiven.

So being a true religion is not at all like being a justified sinner. One is a matter of having true beliefs, and the other is a matter of being forgiven for some wrongdoing. What Barth is probably trying to say is that both are matters of something sinful being turned into something good. In justification, a sinful, 'damned and lost' person becomes a person accepted by God. Religion, which according to Barth is faithless and futile, 'without any aptitude or merit', becomes 'justified by revelation' (112), the mediator of something God-given and life-saving. But forgiving a sin is nothing like turning a false statement into a true one. In fact it is impossible to say how a false statement could be turned into a true one, unless that is a rather misleading way of saying that the false statement will be corrected.

If two statements contradict each other, at least one of them must be false. And if two statements are identical or very similar, they must both be true, or nearly true. It follows that, when a Hindu says 'there is a being of supreme bliss' and when a Christian says the same thing, one statement cannot be false while the other is true, even if God likes one statement and dislikes the other.

I conclude that the use of 'sublimation', to denote a divine act which turns some statement which is false into one which is true, is senseless. I also conclude that if two statements from different religions are virtually identical, they are both either true or false. It cannot be the case that one is false, and the other is true. It is even more obvious that one of them cannot be both false and true, and this makes it clear that truth is very different from justification. A corrected falsehood is not analogous to a justified sinner, because justified sinners go on sinning, whereas corrected truth-claimants do not go on believing what is false.

The Universality of Grace

What Barth wants to do is to preserve the unique truth of Christ at all costs. But what he is in danger of doing is to limit the grace of God to one tiny part of the world's population. The irony is that he also wants Christ to be the saviour of the whole world, and therefore gives the church the mission of evangelising the earth. But such evangelisation will take time, and may never be completed, and it will never manage to save the whole of humanity. A more plausible way in which Christ can be saviour of all is for Christ to act in many faiths and cultures, often in hidden or incomplete ways, but always in ways which can subsequently make salvation available to all. Barth does later say that Christ indeed acts in many faiths and cultures, but he is not prepared to say that they actually make salvation available to all. They just echo the one really true revelation in Jesus Christ.

Yet God's grace is given, as he says, without respect to any aptitude or merit of its recipients. If so, it seems that it could be given in many forms and degrees to the whole earth. Christianity will not be the only 'true religion'. It will be a faith which says that Christ, the eternal Word, is the living and acting saviour of the whole world, and aims to accomplish the reconciliation of the whole world, and indeed the whole universe, to God. For this to be the case, there can be no small group on one small planet which is the only true religion. There will be disclosures of the spiritual truth of creation, sanctification, and union with the creator, in a myriad forms, perhaps on myriads of worlds.[1] But on our world, it is through the traditions based on the disclosure of this truth in and through Jesus that this message has been most clearly proclaimed.

Barth's remarks on Judaism in his third chapter are particularly sad. Having said that Old Testament Judaism was a true vehicle of grace, he now writes that the Jews, when they rejected Jesus, 'defiled the word and the covenant' (116). So modern Judaism is 'a religion rejected, emptied … from which God has turned away his countenance' (117). Whatever Barth said later about Judaism, these words about Judaism as a desublimation, as a return of the tradition to falsehood and faithlessness, and as the withdrawal of grace from what was once said to be an everlasting covenant, recall the ghosts of anti-Judaism which have disgraced Christian history. They also draw attention to the great anxiety of certain Evangelical forms of Christianity that it is possible to lose faith, to have divine grace withdrawn, and to be damned and lost. What to a historian of religion is the reasonable rejection of Jesus as Messiah on the ground that he had not liberated Israel from Rome or brought about a new age of peace and justice, has been turned into the faithless rejection of God by Israel.

We need a better account than Barth's of the place of Judaism and of other religions in the providence of God, given the truth of

---

[1] See Andrew Davis, *Metaphysics of Exo-life* (Grasmere, ID: SacraSage Press, 2023).

the Christian Gospel. Perhaps part of that account will be a greater recognition of the failures of Christianity to be true to its own alleged beliefs in humility, non-violence, and care for all creation. That is, after all, what Barth recognises in calling religion faithless.

But to recognise the failures of all religions is not to say that all religions are completely faithless, and certainly not to say that only one of them is touched by divine grace. If one has faith in divine grace, then one cannot look for less than that it touches all humanity. Grace is not offered to a tiny few, without regard to their merit. It must be offered to all, and we must look harder to see how and where this is so. The tragedy of Barth is that he has a contracted and introverted vision of Christian faith rather than an expansive and outward-looking vision of the inclusion of the whole cosmos in the plan of redemption. Or if he does have that wider vision – and it appears especially in his later writings – how much more important it is that he should renounce his utter condemnation of all religion.

Godlessness and Faith

One of the odd things about Barth's view of religion is his insistence on the importance of the weakness and godlessness of those who are to become Christians. According to some surveys, about 85 per cent of world populations identify with a religion.[2] Barth would presumably think this a very bad thing. Many would expect that it is those with some inclination for religion who are more likely to be interested in Christianity, and might think that some sort of 'religious consciousness' – a sense of a higher power, moral demand, or the mystery of being – would be a good preparation for Christian faith. Barth disagrees. He writes, such views are 'to the dishonour of God and the eternal damnation of souls' (122). So much for people

---

[2] See Pew Research Center, *The Future of World Religions; Population Growth Projections 2010–2050* (Washington, DC: Pew Research Center, 2015).

like me (and, of course, Schleiermacher). He points out that the first Christians boasted only of their weakness, because they had nothing which could count as a qualification for receiving the Gospel. 'The Christian, like Abraham, is the godless one who has been justified' (124). All depends upon unmerited, surprising grace. He cites the publican in the Temple, the prodigal son, the poor Lazarus, and the guilty crucified thief as examples.

Yet these are not examples of godless and worldly persons. Abraham at once responded to God's call to leave Ur, the publican prayed heartily for forgiveness, the prodigal returned to his father, Lazarus and even the guilty thief looked to God for mercy. These were not perfect people, but they were all penitent God-fearers. That was their preparation for the Gospel. Jesus' mission was to the 'lost sheep' of the house of Israel.[3] But his mission was to console them, to promise hope, and call for repentance. They were not sheep who were happy and contented in their godless state. They had lost their way. They needed and wanted a shepherd, but had given up hope of finding one. Their need was deeply felt, and Jesus wished to answer that need. This was a religious need, for love and spiritual leadership. Truly godless people do not have such needs; that is precisely what godlessness is.

Nor did Jesus condemn those who embraced religion without feeling such needs – the brother of the prodigal son received his share of the inheritance. It was only hypocrisy in religion that Jesus condemned, not religion itself, whose laws he accepted.[4] The weakness of early Christians may have been a social fact, but Barth, despite his denial of any factors which might cause people to receive grace, is in danger of accepting this acknowledgment of weakness and lostness as a necessary qualification for conversion and election.

For Barth, the grace of Jesus Christ is seen 'in the spiritual poverty of those who believed in him' (129). He opposes the idea that

---

[3] Matthew 15, 24: 'I was sent only to the lost sheep of the house of Israel.'
[4] Matthew 5, 17.

it is the spiritually advanced who are true Christians, and he insists that it is the spiritually poor, who know they have nothing of value to offer, who are sinners even in their best actions, who are 'wholly and completely opposed to God' (132), who have the true religion.

There is some force in this position, for spiritual pride in one's own superior piety or wisdom is a temptation, not a virtue. Matthew does have Jesus say, 'Blessed are the poor in spirit, for theirs is the kingdom of Heaven.'[5] But it would be odd to interpret this as saying that the godless possess the kingdom of Heaven. It more naturally means that the kingdom belongs to those who are humble, who do not regard themselves with spiritual pride. There is a temptation to flaunt one's spiritual insight, but there is also a temptation to flaunt one's spiritual poverty, to say that one is worth nothing and that one is wholly dependent on God. For that can be a combination of self-loathing and a belief that all one thinks and does is the work of God, which makes one both very humble yet also virtually divine – it is, after all, not I who think and act, but God, on whom I totally depend. And that is as divine as humans can get. Self-abasement is a vice too. One must, after all, love others as one loves oneself, so there is a place for self-love after all. And though one might be wholly dependent on God, one must not confuse one's own actions with God's actions.

The path between spiritual pride and self-loathing is narrow and hard to follow. But I doubt whether a belief that human persons are created in the image of God is really compatible with thinking that they are worth nothing. One may interpret the 'fall of man' as something which obliterates that image (though Barth does not), but the Bible hardly suggests that, and as long as a trace of that image can be found humans are of very great worth. They should be treated with dignity, and they have many creative possibilities to be realised, even if they have been corrupted by evil or unwise choices.

In his later work, Barth affirms that this is the case. Even there, however, there is a suspicion that humans only have creativity and

---

[5] Matthew 5, 3.

dignity because Christ died for them and assumes them into his risen life by sheer grace, and not for any capacities that they inherently possess. Whereas one might think that being created in the divine image is something that all humans share just by virtue of their existence. They share this not only if they have accepted Jesus as their Lord, but just because God has given them the possibilities and gifts that they possess as human beings. Not all humans are weak, godless, and spiritually poor. Being created in God's image, they possess a potentiality for relationship with God, and for strengthening by the Spirit. This is a much more positive view of humanity, and throws doubt on any claim that all humans stand condemned as miserable sinners.

The Fall of Humanity

If one does speak of the fall of man – and I am not sure such an expression is appropriate any longer, since humans have evolved or 'risen' from simpler forms of life – one needs to be careful of what that implies. Even for Jews and also for Eastern Orthodox Christians who take the Genesis account of the expulsion from Eden seriously, there is no such thing as original sin. There were certainly bad consequences for Adam and Eve, and for their descendants (though a long story is needed of how this ancient myth represents a pre-scientific insight into how a natural desire for self-preservation became transformed in the evolution of early hominids into hatred and hostility towards others). But there is no question of guilt for something that happened long before one was born, and present humans are still capable of making good moral choices, however difficult that may be.

Barth speaks as though all humans are depraved, totally sinful, and deserving of the wrath of God and of eternal perdition. Man is the 'enemy of grace' (131). Looking at human history, it certainly seems that hatred, violence, and greed are endemic. However, there are also saints, men and women who give their lives for the sake of goodness, in every culture and religion. The picture seems to be one of a large number of people who are fairly indifferent to morality, a minority who are grossly immoral, and another minority who are morally heroic. It does not look as though all humanity is opposed to God.

Barth says, however, that such opposition only becomes apparent when one sees the suffering of Jesus on the Cross, and realises that it is his death, the death of God, that makes the extent of human opposition to God clear. 'It is God's revelation in Jesus Christ and it alone', he writes, 'by which this characterisation of religion as idolatry and works-righteousness and thus its exposure as faithlessness, can really be carried out' (93). Is that really so obvious, however? Does even the crucifixion entail that all humans are opposed to God? There were, after all, many disciples who loved Jesus. Even if they ran away or, like Peter, denied knowing Jesus, they never killed him or hated him. Jesus certainly died because of the wickedness of humans, but there is no suggestion that all humans were opposed to grace. There were those who heard his call and tried, however feebly, to follow him. Many of them died cruel deaths for their faith. It seems strange to say that all humans are completely opposed to God, when some followed Jesus to death.

Then there is the question of how it is that complete opposition to God can exist when God has created the world as very good. Indeed, if God predestines everything, God has predestined such opposition, and so God is in some sense in opposition to Godself. On the other hand, if God opposes evil with wrath and condemnation, then something other than God must cause evil. Barth's suggestion is that it is man himself, but this gives human freedom power over God, power to do things God hates and punishes. And that is incompatible with Barth's understanding of human freedom, which holds that everything that man does is wholly determined by God.

For me, this has two important implications. First, if God is good, there must be a good reason why God allows humans to determine

their own lives in obedience or in opposition to God and goodness. Though theologians have always found it almost impossible
to know exactly what this is, I guess it must lie in the fact that it is
good for some creatures to be autonomous, to learn and grow in
awareness and understanding, and to choose their own futures to
some extent.

Second, if a God who permits this is good, and loves and cares for
creation, then God's wrath cannot be endless and changeless. God
must make it really possible, and in the end perhaps inevitable, for
all creatures to find some sort of fulfilment in God.

Barth, as a Christian, senses this, and insists that God freely par-
dons and draws sinners to Godself. But if that is so, why does he
need to say that man is 'a sinner even in his best Christian actions'
(131)? It is much more sensible to say that humans are free to do
good or evil, that perhaps all fall prey to evil to some extent, and so
need divine grace to strengthen them; but many succeed in doing
some good, and some really love and do good in heroic ways. This
would avoid the intolerable paradox that God hates humans, and
loves them (or perhaps only some of them?) at the same time. It
would also avoid Barth's intolerant and uncharitable condemnation of all religions as faithless, his antipathy to Enlightenment values such as freedom, equality, and fraternity, and to even the best
aspects of German liberal theology.

A Short History of Christianity Revised

These antipathies are expressed in his extraordinary comment that
'a history of Christianity can only be written as a history of this
problem' (129), namely the problem of Christianity as a religion
of superior wisdom and morality versus Christianity as the site of
unmerited grace given to Godless men and women. The comment
is extraordinary because every historian knows that there are always
many different ways of writing history. It is never true that there is
only one way of writing history. Histories of Christianity have been

written many times, and few of them agree with Barth's account. I will provide a different interpretation, although it will be as brief and cursory as Barth's.

I have noted that Barth sees the earliest stages of Christianity as acknowledging its own weakness and total dependence on sheer grace for any worth it might possess. But even at that stage he holds that Christianity as a religion was already beginning to boast of itself as a superior religion to pagan religions, superior in wisdom and morality, in 'its monotheism, its morality, and its mystery, rather than upon the grace of Jesus Christ' (125). The odd thing is that he thinks this is deplorable. On the contrary, I think it is just true that Christian monotheism was superior to Roman polytheism. There is just one creator God, not many quarrelsome gods. It is just true that Christian morality was superior in many ways to Roman morality. Christians abolished child sacrifice, insisted on love of enemies, and at least tried the experiment of holding all things in common and taking special care of the ill, the poor, and the socially deprived. And it is just true that Christianity offered the hope of the triumph of love in a world which seemed to be collapsing into war and chaos. I find it hard to think that Christians could think otherwise. I see no reason why such facts should be incompatible with thinking that humans are wholly dependent upon God, and depend solely on divine grace if their sins, which are many if not total, are to be forgiven, and if they are to share in the divine nature.

It is not boastful to recognise that such things are true, and no one needs to be spiritually weak, burdened with a sense of sin, or completely opposed to God before they can receive God's saving grace. The disciples on the whole were actually looking for a Messianic saviour to be sent from God, and they worshipped in the Temple, and so were surely part of that 'saving remnant' of Judaism which Barth admits were already recipients of divine grace. And it was those who were spiritually perceptive and morally serious who were open to the preaching of the Gospel.

Of course I would not hold that one has to be an intellectual or saint in order to be a Christian. The love of God in Christ can be received by the simplest person and the greatest sinner. But one is not debarred from faith if one is strong in prayer, in good works, and in a longing for God. Jesus' parable in Matthew 25, of the sheep and the goats, makes it clear that the sheep are people who do good works, and the goats are people who ignore morality. In that parable, faith in God or in Christ is not mentioned. That does not mean that moral goodness of itself will unite one with the divine nature. But it does mean that being morally strong is not a barrier to faith, but rather a stepping stone to faith. So I think Barth is simply wrong about this. A strong sense of sin can be a failure to perceive the goodness of the image of God in human beings. It is something which Christian faith should remove, something which prevents one from seeing other people as loved, not hated, by God, and as destined for glory. A crippling sense of sin is something which some people have, but I would not recommend it, and would instead encourage people to see the work of God in the potentialities of every human being, and not to view them as 'enemies of grace'.

The Medieval Synthesis

When Christianity became the official religion of the Roman Empire, Barth says that it embraced worldly political aims, claiming eventually even to be 'the first and true world power'. It 'formed itself into a specific universal intellectual–moral–aesthetic, worldly configuration' (125), and thus became 'A witness to the glory of Western man' rather than to God. Any modern historian would agree that there were many misuses of power and shameful episodes in the life of the medieval churches. But they would probably also add that the monasteries were formative in reviving education and learning, as well as being foremost in charitable works, building hospitals and schools. It was a mixed record, but that is very differ-ent from condemning it as contradicting the grace of God.

The work of the thirteenth-century theologian Thomas Aquinas used the philosophy of Aristotle to construct an impressive sys-tematic and philosophically acute account of the Christian faith. But why should that be called a 'worldly configuration' rather than what it is, an account of the world in the light of the doctrines of creation and redemption by a perfect and loving God? One could well call Barth's own prolix theology a worldly configuration, since it attempts much the same thing, being a human intellectual con-struction of great rhetorical power to present the world in the light of God's revelation in Christ. It is a good thing that Christianity can be laid out as intellectually coherent and enlightening, and that an account of the distinctive virtues of humanity can be given which culminate in the hope of the vision of God.

It is an unusual perspective which sees Thomist theology as a witness to the glory of Western man, when what it does is to set out what it means for humans to be wholly dependent creatures of God who are destined to be redeemed in Christ. I suppose this sort of theology was framed in a Western conceptual tradition (as is Barth's), and it did sometimes fall into the trap of confusing some Western cultural norms with universal Christian truth. It was its failure to accommodate to more Eastern traditions which partly accounts for its failure to penetrate into India and China, and also for its failure to resist the advances of Islam in previously Christian lands. It was not so much the assimilation of Christian faith to cul-ture that was its problem. It was the failure to adapt to different and changing cultures which weakened it. I would therefore be inclined to turn Barth's view on its head, and say that more assim-ilation to different cultures is what Christianity needs, rather than an attempted condemnation of all cultures.

Just imagine what Protestant Reformed Christianity means in the rich and syncretistic culture of East Asia. It means the intrusion of colonialist and alien Western ideas into the rich, ancient, and diverse religious world of Asia, with the introduction of arguments about the Trinity, the Incarnation, and the church which have no resonance at all with Asian ideas, which ideas Protestant missionaries in any case have tended to regard as pagan superstitions. That is not a good recipe for preaching that Christ is the saviour of the world and the fulfilment of the religious hopes of all the world. But then of course Barth thinks that is a good thing, since he does not see Christ as the fulfilment of worldly culture, but as its nemesis.

'Modern Man'

When it comes to the Reformation and Renaissance, Barth reaches a peak of condemnation. 'Man', he says, 'discovers himself' (126), and finds that he does not need religion, except possibly as 'a useful force for education and order' (127). Modern man, he says, relies on himself to form and achieve the goals that he sets for himself. In fact he reduces the church to a voluntary society for supporting the highest ideals of modern man, the servant of ever-changing social and political forces. Not realising that 'the Christian is strong only in his weakness', even Christians prove themselves to be 'the enemies of grace' (131), and to be in complete contradiction to God's revelation.

Barth here propounds a stereotype of 'modern man' as being wholly self-sufficient, as inventing his own moral ideals, and as being one who 'firmly relies on himself' (128). It is as though Barth sees modern man as rebelliously rejecting God and making himself the master of his own destiny.

The story is much more complicated than this. From the seventeenth century the Aristotelian picture of nature fell away, as modern science came to see the world in a very different light. There were well-known controversies about the Genesis creation story and about evolution. Added to this, the development of critical history meant that the Biblical documents were subjected to closer and less dogmatically constrained analysis, which tended to throw their inerrancy in doubt. New philosophical approaches focussed more on the nature of human existence and consciousness, and split into Idealist, Empiricist, and materialist sects. After the French Revolution, there came to be an emphasis on universal human rights, which, in France especially, caused criticism of the churches as reactionary and socially divisive institutions. And, as world travel and trade grew, there was much more contact with, and understanding of, other cultures and religions.

All these factors led to new understandings of the world, and to more freely expressed criticisms of institutions, like most churches, that were felt to be rooted still in past ideologies. Add to this the Protestant Reformation, and it became apparent that Christendom, the acceptance of one all-embracing Christian ideology in Europe, was ended. Barth's Protestant theology was part of this revolution.

Barth is in fact a 'modern man', critical of church tradition, brought up in the German Idealist and liberal schools, reacting against the alliance of many German churches with the Nazi Party, and advocating a revolutionary theology of total depravity, unmerited grace, the sole and complete truth of the Bible, the necessity of faith in Jesus Christ alone for salvation, and rejection of good works and obedience to the Catholic Magisterium as a religiously effective means of grace.

Like many revolutionaries, Barth liked to claim that his views had always been present in Christianity, and in fact had always been its living heart, although often hidden or repressed by the authorities. I would suggest another reading of history. Christianity began as a Jewish Messianic sect, with belief in an early return of the Messiah in glory to judge the world and usher in a new age of justice and peace. It has changed markedly many times, and it has always contained many diverse interpretations of what the Messiah is, and of what exactly the hope for the final fulfilment for God's purpose for the world is.[6]

---

[6] My account of changes in Christian history is given in my *Re-thinking Christianity*.

The medieval world adopted a broadly Johannine idea of the Messiah as a fully divine Incarnation, who still lives 'in Heaven', and who had founded the Catholic church as a means of uniting humans to the Messiah and bringing them to live for ever in Heaven. For many medieval Christians, the Messiah becomes the saviour not just of Jews but of the whole world. He will return at an indeterminate time, and divide humans into those who suffer in Hell for ever, and those who live in the presence of God for ever.

Human Fulfilment and Liberal Christianity

In the modern age, from about the seventeenth century in Europe, the authority of the Catholic church was questioned, as it was widely felt to be corrupt in many ways. This inevitably, though to the dismay of many Protestants, led to questioning the authority of the Bible, which had after all been compiled by the church. It also led to acceptance of freedom of belief and of conscience. Once people felt free to criticise and form their own beliefs, many different interpretations of Christianity sprang up, including interpretations which saw it as anti-scientific and socially repressive. I am inclined to the view that these radical interpretations were often well-founded. There was no revolt against God. There was rather the growth of honest doubt about whether there was a God, or whether any church or Biblical authority could be trusted. Doubts were openly expressed about whether a loving God could send anyone to Hell for ever, about whether only those who were baptised could go to Heaven, about how a man could really be God, and about whether Jesus would really return to earth in the near future. Liberal forms of Christianity were born.

Liberalism is not wholly a matter of doubt, by any means. It accepts the main findings of modern science about the size and age of the universe, and about the evolutionary emergence of humanity, and that entails expanding and revising obsolete beliefs that only Jesus of Nazareth, on this small and peripheral planet, could be the saviour of the whole cosmos, and that the cosmos might end when he comes to earth on the clouds in a few years' time. This can lead to an expansion of thought about the extent of God's power, about the way in which the eternal Christ is present in Jesus, and about the universal goal of union 'in Christ' which must now be seen as beyond this space-time.

Liberal Christianity also expresses positive moral insights, claiming that divine love entails a divine desire for universal fulfilment and happiness, and that strict retributive justice is not compatible with love even of the unrighteous, and therefore needs to be replaced by a more reformative view of justice. This means asking what really makes for human fulfilment – not a goal and purpose 'that man has independently chosen' (128), but the objective ideal of a loving creator God. And it means asking whether a powerful and wise God would really create beings whom God would cause to suffer in Hell without hope of release.

There are moral truths about human fulfilment that are implicit in the Christian doctrines of creation and redemption and are eternally rooted in the mind of God. They do not depend on acceptance of the Christian faith or membership of a Christian church, and to uncover them is to have expanded and deepened the range of moral consideration further than many Christians have managed to do. If morality is part of Christian faith – and righteousness is a key theme throughout the Bible – then modernity has deepened Christian faith in at least one important respect. It has focussed attention on the welfare and fulfilment of human life. This focus can and should exist within religious forms of life, both as a critique of practices that curtail human freedom, equality, and dignity, and as an ideal goal of religious life. It did so in the work of the Christian humanist Erasmus, but Barth would as usual, at least at this stage of his life, call even Erasmus' best work faithless and sinful.

Christians have always theoretically supposed that the two Christian major ethical principles are love of God and of humanity.

So they can hardly be opposed to programmes aiming at human happiness and the promotion of many forms of human excellence. What they have not always accepted is that such ideals should be realised in earthly life, not just in Paradise, and that they have rather definite social and political implications.

Although Jesus is not recorded as having made many references to political matters, there is no doubt that he showed compassion for the poor and socially deprived, and that he proclaimed the coming of a kingdom in which all would be free from greed and hatred. The very first Christians held all things in common, and had special concern for widows and orphans. In the Old Testament it is even clearer that freedom from slavery and from domination by tyrannical military powers was a great good for Israel, and therefore, when it was thought through, for all people – even if slavery as a social practice was not abandoned, and the equality of men and women had by no means been even aimed for.

Where there are obligations to treat others with respect and compassion, one may speak of the rights of all to be so treated. So human rights should have always been important in religion. Nevertheless, the eighteenth-century insistence on human rights was often seen as dangerously revolutionary and opposed to good order in society. In Europe it was often seen as opposed to the necessity to defend the truth of the Christian faith, and to the belief that humans had no rights before God, who disposed all things by divine will, and whose revealed will was unquestionable.

It is preferable to proclaim that God's will is not arbitrary, but is ordered to good, and therefore to universal fulfilment and happiness, than to say that such things are somehow opposed to Christian faith. Love of God, love of wisdom, beauty, and truth, and love of humanity are intertwined; therefore true humanism – concern for the flourishing of human lives and for the exercise of human intellectual and moral virtues – is a religious duty.

It must be said that Barth understood the social implications of Christian teaching very well – not for nothing was he known as the 'red pastor' in his early parish. He emphasised these implications more fully in his later writings. Yet his negative reaction to the secularism of the Enlightenment led to a dominating emphasis on the universality and totality of human sin.

If my short history of Christianity is anywhere near the truth, it is highly unlikely that 'the Christian is strong only in his weakness' (130), or that 'man is a sinner even in his best Christian actions' (131). Sin is the corruption of humanity, and it is what alienates all humans from God. But all humans can be strong in wisdom and love, and Christians can be strong in faith and hope. Humans may, and should, rely on the grace of God to perfect their wisdom, love, and faith, and to unite them to the divine nature. But there is no need for them to grovel in the dust and continually confess their weaknesses with mournful cries. They should, Christian or not, pursue virtue and happiness with all their strength. Christians have the advantage, if they are right, that their pursuit will meet with success, with the aid of a power beyond their own, leading towards the perfection to which God calls them.

Peniel

Barth spends a little time expounding the story of Jacob wrestling with an angel at the Jabbok river.[7] This is one of the most mysterious episodes in the Old Testament, and its interpretation is much disputed. Some scholars say that it was originally a story about Jacob wrestling with a river spirit who challenged him as he crossed the river into Canaan. But as it stands, it is a story of wrestling with an angel or even with a manifestation of God, which lasted all night until daybreak, when the angel dislocated Jacob's hip. Jacob did not submit, but asked for the angel's blessing. The angel blessed him, and gave him the new name 'Israel', which could be translated as 'God contends'.

---

[7] Genesis 32, 22f.

Barth holds that wrestling with God shows that humans are enemies of God, thus supporting his view that man as such 'stands wholly and completely opposed to God' (132). Nevertheless, man prevails despite his weakness, and is blessed by God even in his opposition (man is a justified sinner), and God's face is revealed. This Peniel, says Barth, can be taken to mean Protestant Reformed Christianity, in which pure grace reveals God's face even to those who fight against him, and that form of Christianity thereby 'becomes the true religion' (132).

This is obviously not an interpretation any Jew could give. Nor does the story seem to show that man is faithless and weak. On the contrary, Jacob is so strong that he wrestles all night and eventually prevails. He was about to cross the river into the Promised Land and, far from rejecting God, had obeyed God's command to do so.[8] It is hard to interpret what is meant by wrestling with God and prevailing over God. But 'wrestling with God' is probably not what the faithless enemies of grace do. It is more like what those do who believe in God, but must work and pray persistently to discover God's will, or even to persuade God to do what one desires (to bless Jacob as he passes into the Promised Land). To prevail over God may be to have one's hopes and prayers answered, but only after long and persistent endeavour.

This interpretation would be reminiscent of Jesus' equally mysterious parable of the widow and the unjust judge,[9] when the widow's persistence in prayer moved even an unjust judge to grant her request. I do not claim to have uncovered the correct interpretation, if it even makes sense to ask for such a thing. But I do think that there is no reason for thinking that the story shows that man is the enemy of God (Jacob is obeying God, and asking for blessing from God), and there is no reason for thinking that it shows one version of Protestant Christianity (which is supposed to hold that

---

[8] Genesis 31, 3.
[9] Luke 18, 1–8.

God justifies even God's enemies) to be the true religion. It might, however, suggest that persistence in prayer and action can prevail upon God to bless what the faithful undertake.

There is also, in Barth's comments, an unfortunate confusion between grace and truth. He argues that it is not because of the immanent truth of a particular religion of grace that one religion becomes the true one. It is 'the reality of grace itself' which makes something a religion of grace (133). This argument needs careful unpicking. First of all, it is totally unclear what 'immanent truth' might be. A proposition is either true or false (though it could be partly true or false if it is not quite clear). It is logically inept to call any religion true; but it is doubly inept to call anything immanently true. I suppose 'immanent' means 'in itself', or not made true by something else. But propositions are made true by facts, or states of affairs. If we could call a religion, or to be more exact, a proposition or set of propositions in a specific religion, true, we would be saying that some state of affairs in the real world makes them true. Things are as a proposition says they are. In that case, to say a proposition in religion is immanently true would be to say that there is some state of affairs in the world which makes it true, and its truth is not just a conclusion from some other state of affairs. Then we might say that some propositions of a particular religion of grace are made true by some states of affairs – things are as they are said to be in these propositions, and they do not just follow as inferences from other propositions.

Now that we have clarified what might be meant by this, we can see that it does not differ at all from saying that the reality of grace (that is, the fact that there really is in the world an act of divine grace) makes something a religion of grace. It is just a slightly different way of saying the same thing – that a true religion of grace is one that accurately states that there really are acts of grace in the world, and that conveys such acts of grace. There is no difference, logically, between saying that the truth of a religion of grace makes a religion the true one, which Barth denies (133), and saying that the reality of grace makes a religion the true one (which Barth affirms). I guess that what Barth means to say is that you can have religions which claim to be based on grace, but are not in fact channels of grace. And you can have religions which are in fact channels of grace, correctly described as the grace of the God revealed in Jesus Christ. In other words, some religions make claims about grace which are not completely true.

In fact Barth says that 'no religion is true. A religion can only become true' (111). Unfortunately, this does not make sense, because if a religion ever becomes true, then from that point on it simply is true. And Barth is quite clear that 'the Christian religion is the true religion' (112). It turns out, says, Barth, that only Protestant religion is true, even when Protestantism is 'an especially emphatic rebellion against grace' (133).

Even if this, God forbid, were the case, it still falls into one more logical error. Barth says, 'the religion of grace can be made into the true religion only by grace itself' (133). Grace is the free act of God by which sins are forgiven and humans are made righteous by God – I do not disagree with Barth about that. A religion of grace is a religion which claims that God, or some higher spiritual power, forgives sins and frees humans from the power of sin. What Barth holds entails that such claims are false. Yet he also holds that there is one, and only one, subset of Christianity which truly conveys the grace of God. But even if it were the case that only this religion could forgive sin, it still would not make this religion true, for the simple reason that persons can be forgiven and freed from sin even though they still believe many false things. You would have to be right, perhaps, about the existence and power of grace. But you can be wrong about, for example, the age of the universe, the return of Jesus to this planet in the future, or the nature of the Trinity. You can be wrong about quite a lot of things. Even when receiving true grace from God, your religion might not be true, if that means that all its official pronouncements are true (they say what is the case).

That might raise the possibility that even Protestants can be wrong about many things – so their religion is not wholly true – and still be authentic channels of grace. That, in turn, raises the possibility that there might be authentic channels of grace which are wrong about a great many things, though they will still have the main thing needful, the free forgiveness of sin and the empowering help of a higher spiritual reality.

9 | Universal Grace

Religions and Grace

Barth now at last turns to consider two religions in slightly more detail, providing an analysis of two related Japanese Buddhist religions, Jodo-Shin and Jodo-Shin-Shu. These are religions of pure grace, centred on Amida Buddha, the creator and lord of a Pure Land in the west. Amida will grant forgiveness of sins and a place in the Pure Land if devotees have faith in him. These religions have many things in common with Christianity, and they are certainly religions of grace. They could well be channels of grace, even though they would, according to Christians, have some false doctrines, like reincarnation, denial of one personal and morally demanding creator God, an incarnation of God, and the final union of all things in Christ, the eternal Word of God.

But Barth refuses to say that they are genuine channels of grace. Such Buddhist religions, he says, stand or fall on the validity of 'a passionate human desire for a redemption through dissolution, for entry into Nirvana' (138). This is a strange charge, since one major strand of Buddhist thought is that passionate human desires are the cause of suffering in the world, and all attachments to them must be eliminated. Barth says that 'this goal of human desire … is the real governing and determining force' of Buddhism. That is simply the opposite of the truth. It may be that at one level Buddhists hope for a better reincarnation in the Pure Land, just as many Christians hope for Paradise, which could also be said to be a passionate and selfish human desire. But authentic Buddhist teaching is that of 'no-self'. It aims to eliminate any desire for the continued existence of an immortal self.

From a Christian point of view, Buddhism contains many false beliefs, though as I have argued it would be misleading to call it a false religion. It also has beliefs which are analogous to some Christian beliefs, and it arguably is more successful at offering techniques for attaining mindfulness, wisdom, and compassion for all beings than does Christianity.

A very important thing to bear in mind is that religions are not just sets of beliefs. They also often promote contemplation, devotion to personal gods, and demanding moral principles and virtues. The Indian traditions call these the three ways (yogas) of wisdom, devotion, and action (jnana, bhakti, and karma). Different religions emphasise these elements to different degrees. Christianity stresses devotion, and thinks of 'grace' as the inward and active power of the divine Spirit in human lives. Buddhism, in most forms, stresses wisdom, renunciation, and the practice of compassion. At popular levels, there can be devotion to gods or Buddhas, but there is no supreme God to judge, forgive, or empower human lives.

Does this mean there is no grace in Buddhism, as Barth holds? That is not an easy question to answer. I think that if God is universally loving, as Christians claim, then God will be present everywhere to enhance good and frustrate evil. The sincere pursuit of good will then in fact always be enhanced by God, even if that enhancement is not recognised for what it is. We are all aware that when we seek to do justice by our own power, we are not in fact totally self-sustaining. The example and encouragement of others, and the very ability and opportunity to be just, are not within our own power. This is why, in the Buddhist world, the serious pursuit of liberation is to be pursued in the monastic life, which helps monks to exercise their own powers more effectively, and why it is considered important to have a personal spiritual guide. A Christian can see the grace of God at work in the communities of

Buddhist monks, as they seek to renounce selfish desire and pursue the liberation not just of themselves, but of all beings.

These are religious practices, because they are found in communities which seek to renounce worldly attachments, accept that the cosmos is, by the laws of karma, ordered to the destruction of evil and the promotion of good, and because members of those communities seek for all an ultimate goal of nirvana, a non-material state of indescribable wisdom and compassion. They have no doctrine of divine grace, but it is unacceptable to describe them as 'poor, utterly lost, pagans', as Barth does (140).

The two Buddhist schools that Barth briefly describes belong to an extreme form of a tradition, the Mahayana, which introduces the idea of bodhisattvas, beings who postpone their own liberation until all beings are liberated from suffering, and who bring to the Pure Land all who have faith in them. Thereby the element of devotion is introduced into Buddhism, and this, as Barth says, looks much more like Christianity. It still, Christians would think, has some false beliefs, but these do not destroy the possibility that forgiving and perfecting spiritual power is found in them.

Barth simply denies this, saying that Christians 'believe Jesus Christ and no other to be grace and truth' (141). There is a sense in which I think this is true – ultimately, the eternal Christ who was incarnate in Jesus is the source of divine forgiveness and empowerment for all humans without exception. But there is a sense in which it is false – God's grace, according to Christians fully expressed in its true nature in Jesus, is given to all humans in many forms, wherever goodness, devotion, and wisdom are genuinely sought.

This is actually admitted by Barth, when he accepts pre-Christian Judaism, which had no knowledge of Jesus, as a channel of divine grace. I have called this 'incomplete grace' (though I am not very happy with the term), but if God's grace is truly for all, then it must be present throughout the world. Even secularists, who honestly believe there is no God, but who pursue truth, beauty, and goodness, must be touched by God's grace, though they do not recognise it as such.

There are forms of religion, too, like Confucianism, which have little or no sense of possible relationship to conscious spiritual beings like God, but are committed to ways of life which reflect the true order of things, the 'way of Heaven'. That idea, that goodness is rooted in the ultimate nature of things, I regard as a primary element of religious belief. It means that I do not regard all humans as essentially evil, damned, and opposed to God. I do not regard grace as given to some humans without any regard to their merit or aspirations and actions. And I do not confine the loving and reconciling actions of God to one small religious group.

To put those points more positively, I think that humans are created to co-operate with God in bringing new creative values into being. Humans fail to be totally truthful, creative, and loving, but they can and should try their best to become so. I believe that when they do, God's grace will forgive their failures, empower their actions, and ultimately bring all who consent to share in the wisdom, beauty, and beatitude of the divine nature. God's grace, like God's love, is not limited to one group of humans. It is universally present, though its true nature and power are revealed in the person of Jesus and, however fitfully, in the churches which call him Lord.

I have noted that in later writings Barth comes very near to saying this. He seems to recognise that his early condemnations of religion are brutal and insensitive, and that God's grace is not confined to versions of the Christian religion. But he is unable fully to endorse the presence of saving grace in other faiths – such faiths can only dimly reflect imperfect understandings of Christian truth. They cannot lead to God, and often do not even claim to do so, and so cannot in themselves lead to salvation. He cannot ascribe any meritorious action, in prayer, meditation, and devotion, for example, to the devotees of other faiths, which would enable them actively to co-operate in their journey towards spiritual fulfilment. Therefore he is unable to give any coherent account of how their incomplete grasp of divine grace and truth could be made complete and truthful.

I suspect that this could be accomplished only by a more complete break with the assertions of *Church Dogmatics*, volume I, part 2. This would require an explicit recognition that there is not one faith that contains (or is 'the site' of) the exhaustive fulness of truth, and also that humans can begin to work towards their spiritual fulfilment (their salvation) by their own creative and exploratory responses to the divine.

One of the clearest cases of the presence of divine grace in non-Christian religions is to be found not in Jodo-Shin-Shu but in Hinduism, which Barth does mention, but only to dismiss it in a derogatory way. There are many forms of Hinduism, but one major form is the bhakti schools, which often follow the teaching of Ramanuja. They are often so similar to Christianity that they have been called 'the Methodists of India'. Krishna is an avatar, an earthly appearance of Vishnu, or sometimes himself the Supreme Lord. By loving devotion to Krishna, one may obtain life in his presence, in a spiritual realm. In the Bhagavadgita it says (in Geoffrey Parrinder's verse translation) 'Even a very evil-doer who just loves me with all his might must be reckoned with the righteous.'[1] That could have been written by John Wesley, but he would have attributed the words to Jesus!

The Gita is a spiritual work of great profundity and complexity, written before the New Testament, but all Barth says about it is that one might read it 'with a somewhat blunted sensibility' (139). 'It would be a very poor variety of Evangelical Christianity indeed that could feel an attractive kinship' to such a faith, he says. I have to confess that I share this apparently 'blunted sensibility'! He claims that in bhakti, faith provides a very uncertain idea of God, the replacement of faith by love, and the 'utter formlessness in all respects' of this concept of love. It is really sad to see such a

---

[1] *Bhagavad Gita*, chapter 9, verse 30.

dismissal of one of the great works of human spiritual writing. In fact the idea of God is spelled out at great length, faith in Krishna is included in, not replaced, by love, and the forms of love are painstakingly expounded in some detail. Barth simply cannot have read this material carefully, or met any Indian devotees of Krishna. To include such prejudiced comments in a chapter meant to be about religion is shameful.

A good antidote by a Christian writer is *The Unknown Christ of Hinduism*, by Raimon Panikkar,[2] who, as a Catholic priest (who may therefore not be a member of 'the true religion'), is in no doubt that Krishna is a channel of the grace of God, although it is really not the largely mythological Krishna, according to Panikkar, but the unknown eternal Christ at work).

Universalism

Most commentators on Barth's theology have remarked that in his later work he seems to be, or almost to be, a universalist, believing that all humans will be saved, because humanity as a whole has been united to God in Christ. This would seem to entail that Christianity, which is accepted only by a minority of the world's population, is not the only way to salvation. I will suggest that though he did develop his theological views, which is only natural, he did not decisively reject them but rather chose to emphasise different aspects which had always been there, and to correct some rhetorical and polemical exaggerations in the way he had stated his opposition to German liberal religion. However, I will also suggest that he did not manage fully to integrate his earlier and later emphases, and to that extent unresolved tensions continue to exist in his theology.

Even within *Dogmatics*, volume I, part 2, Barth speaks of God as being 'against and for all men, the whole of humanity' (159). That

[2] Raimon Panikkar, *The Unknown Christ of Hinduism* (Maryknoll: Orbis, 1981).

sounds as if no humans are excluded from God's saving embrace, which is given to all without exception.

Remarks suggestive of universalism are repeated more than once later in the *Dogmatics*. In volume II, part 2, Barth writes, 'Before all created reality … the eternal divine decision as such has as its object and content the existence of this one created being, the man Jesus of Nazareth … in and with the existence of this man the eternal divine decision has as its object and content the execution of the divine covenant with man, the salvation of all men.'[3]

God's decision to create Jesus somehow includes the decision to save all men (all humans). The Bible records that Jesus died to save humans. But did he die to save only those who believed in him? This view seems to be in the New Testament.[4] Or did he die to save all people, whether they had heard of him, or hated him, or completely rejected him, or were wholly evil and sinful? Barth's view is, it must be said, not clear. The former option sounds very limiting, since most humans who have existed have never even heard of Jesus. But the latter option sounds like an over-ruling of human freedom, an ignoring of human evil, and a countermanding of the decisions of those who have no desire to be saved if it means submitting to Jesus.

In view of that, it is very difficult to decide whether Barth's phrase 'the salvation of all men' implies simply that God makes this a possibility for all, and one that God desires to be made actual, though God does not compel people to make it actual, or whether it means God will actually save everyone.

The latter option seems to be affirmed when Barth writes, 'To be a creature means to be determined to this end [to share in the overflowing of His own fulness of life and love], to be affirmed, elected, and accepted by God.'[5] Yet again it is possible that 'to be determined'

---

[3] *Church Dogmatics*, volume II, part 2, p. 116.
[4] John 15, 6: 'Whoever does not abide in me is thrown away … thrown into the fire and burned.'
[5] Barth, *Church Dogmatics*, volume III, part 1, p. 364.

may imply that this is what God intends, though God does not ensure that it happens, or whether it means that all humans will actually be elected and accepted by God. The ambiguity remains.

Another relevant phrase to be found in the *Dogmatics* is 'what God has done and revealed in Jesus Christ, namely, the liberation of all men'.[6] That seems to claim that God has revealed in Jesus that all humans will be liberated. It is certainly a very positive Gospel. However, it remains possible that all Barth means to say is that what God has done in Christ is to reveal God's will (desire) to liberate all humans. That is indeed significant, for it entails that God does not will to damn anyone – and that God wills to damn the unjust is a view widely attributed to Calvin. But God wishing to save all humans is not quite universalism.

A more compelling statement Barth makes is that 'there is no-one who is not raised and exalted with Him [Jesus] to true humanity'.[7] Yet even this is not totally clear. All humans might be raised to true humanity in that, because of Jesus' resurrection, they become objects of respect and esteem, in this life. But it may not mean that they will share for ever in God's life and love, which is full salvation. After all, the phrase from Paul's first letter to the Corinthians, 'as all die in Adam, so all will be made alive in Christ',[8] has not usually been taken to entail universal salvation by Christian churches. The second occurrence of the word 'all' has widely been taken to refer only to those who consciously believe in Christ. So it could be in Barth.

The case for Barth's universalism, while quite strong, is not completely compelling. That case, however, does not rest solely on scattered comments throughout the *Dogmatics*. It is explicitly discussed in his 1956 lecture, 'The Humanity of God'. In that lecture Barth announces what he calls a change in his thinking. He writes that, since in Jesus God had united humanity to divinity, God has formed

[6] Ibid., volume IV, part 3, p. 675.
[7] Ibid., volume IV, part 2, p. 271.
[8] 1 Corinthians 15, 22.

a partnership between humanity and God. Whereas in *Dogmatics* volume I, part 1 he had stressed that God was 'wholly Other' than human nature, its thoughts and feelings, he now wished to stress that, because of the Incarnation, human nature has been sanctified by God. It has been united to God. In fact he wrote, 'God's deity includes His humanity.'[9] He even says, 'Deity encloses humanity', and that 'God does not exist without man.'[10]

Perhaps God would not be God without humans, and their history would in fact also be part of the history of God. In a sense he does mean this. For God would not be suffering, loving, and redeeming in the way that God is without the existence of something like humans. God has a history in time when God acts and responds to human actions in the Incarnation. And God has the goal of bringing humans into a fully conscious and loving fellowship with the divine life.

At this point, with supreme irony, Barth comes very near to the Hegelian thesis that the Supreme Spirit generates a world of 'others', by relationship to which it expresses its own nature in a special way. Through a long process of historical development Spirit achieves the destined goal of uniting those 'others' to itself. The dedicated anti-metaphysician at this point after all echoes the world-view of the arch-metaphysician.

Perhaps that is why Barth is so insistent that creation is a free personal act, not a metaphysical principle, which he thinks is the Hegelian position. But there is actually little difference. Hegel, after all, claimed to be a Lutheran, and the first properly Christian, philosopher who put into philosophical language a Trinitarian view of God.[11]

---

[9] Barth, *The Humanity of God*, p. 46.

[10] Ibid., p. 50.

[11] See Hegel, *Lectures on the Philosophy of Religion*, vol. I, p. 84: 'the perfect, absolute religion, in which it is revealed what Spirit, what God is; this is the Christian religion'. I have given an account of this part of Hegel's thought in my *Religion in the Modern World*, pp. 103ff.

Whether or not this is a fair comment, Barth means to say that one should not be pessimistic or cynical or despairing about humanity. There is a place for celebrating the value of human life and endeavour. God 'esteems man highly',[12] and we can do no less. This does seem to be at least a change of emphasis, from thinking of humans as sinners worthy of damnation to thinking of humans as esteemed by God and destined for fellowship with God. And it does seem that all humans are included in this esteem, which is due to 'every living being which bears the human countenance'.[13] One should certainly not hate humanity, but regard all persons as supremely valuable, inasmuch as they are those for whom Christ himself had died, with whom God desires partnership. It follows, says Barth, that 'we have to think of *every human being* [emphasis in the original], even the oddest, most villainous or miserable, as one to whom Jesus Christ is Brother and God is Father … humanity is not blotted out through the fall of man, nor is its goodness diminished'.[14]

This is a strong affirmation of goodness in human nature which, if not innate, is nevertheless ascribed to all humans without exception by God. But is it a declaration of universal salvation? I do not think so. It is saying that one should esteem all humans because they are those for whom Christ died, and for whom God wills eternal life and partnership with God. This gives them rights and dignity, and it 'extends also to everything with which man is endowed',[15] to all aspects of human culture in music, the arts and sciences, and moral sensibility. But it does not say that they will all actually have eternal life with God, even though God desires them to do so.

Indeed, Barth reiterates some of the points he made so strongly in the *Church Dogmatics*, saying that humans have 'a perverted attitude towards God', and that 'man is not good but rather a

[12] Barth, *The Humanity of God*, p. 51.
[13] Ibid., p. 52.
[14] Ibid., p. 53.
[15] Ibid., p. 54.

downright monster'.[16] Barth did not withdraw, but re-emphasised, his claim that God said a decisive 'No' to humans as sinners, as well as a decisive 'Yes' to them as redeemed by God.

Barth holds that 'man is a downright monster' and that 'man is esteemed by God' at the same time. This looks like a blunt contradiction. It can only be saved from contradiction if it can be held that there are different respects in which man is bad and in which man is esteemed by God. This is fairly easily done. In his actual conduct, man is a monster, and deserves punishment. But, as having his punishment taken on by Jesus, and thus as being declared innocent, and as being sanctified by the Holy Spirit, man is esteemed by God.

Unfortunately, this is too easily done. Man as he is, as he makes himself, deserves and receives condemnation. It is man as he is forgiven and sanctified by God who is esteemed. But this means that God does not see, or that God pays no regard to, man as he is (actually, we should remember that God made 'man as he is', which is a complication). God pays regard only to man as he is shaped entirely by God, so God is esteeming His own work, created not by human work or effort, but solely by the free and unmerited grace of God. In fact God esteems His own work in regarding man as righteous, when man is actually a monster.

I would have thought that, on the contrary, God, having the greatest possible degree of knowledge, always sees things as they really are, and cannot really see man as righteous when man is not even good. God would be deceiving himself, in regarding sinners as just when they are not. That cannot be right.

It may seem that there is no justifiable way in which man can be condemned for sin and esteemed for righteousness at the same time. But there is a more obvious solution to this problem. Man could be partly, but not wholly, sinful, and partly, but not wholly righteous, and he could, if only with the help of God, gradually decrease in sinfulness and grow in righteousness. In that case, it

---

[16] Ibid.

could be said that he was condemned for some things and esteemed for others.

It is part of Christian faith to say that humans are not able to free themselves from the tyranny of sin, but that does not mean that they can do no good or that they should never be praised for moral and spiritual efforts. The Gospel of Jesus begins with the word 'Repent',[17] and what is required is that people show regret for their failings. This entails trying to make restitution, where that is possible, resolving to avoid sin in future, and, most importantly, asking for divine help in growing in goodness.

Faith is a matter of trusting that God will help, but there is no instantaneous perfection. There is usually at best a slow and per-haps stumbling growth in the fruits of the Spirit.[18] But there are fruits, and there is growth, and human endeavour in co-operation with the Spirit's inward action will make a real difference in the believer's life.

God will continue to condemn sin, but will also empower a growth in goodness, and give a sure hope that such growth will eventually result in the fruition of conscious loving relationship to a clearly known God.

On such a view, God does not condemn and esteem us at the same time in the same respects. God condemns sin, but also for-gives sin on condition that we are penitent, remorseful, and recep-tive to the power of the Holy Spirit. The penalty of spiritual death or of permanent exclusion from the presence of God is remitted. But, as the doctrine of Purgatory was later to put it, there will be a 'fire of purification' which is a finite penalty for sin that remains. God's forgiveness assures us that the penalty will end, if and insofar as we truly repent. God will empower the penitent with the Spirit, and promises that this empowerment can end with perfect fellowship

---

[17] Matthew 4, 12.

[18] Galatians 5, 22. The fruits of the Spirit are: 'love, joy, peace. Patience, kindness, generosity, faithfulness, gentleness, and self-control'.

with God. Thus God will value us and our works and thoughts, because of the partnership that is now begun in us, and is able to unite us to the divine at last.

This account avoids the apparent contradiction of God seeing man as righteous when man is not. And it affirms that forgiveness is offered to all without exception.

The Final Position?

This account, however, involves some major consequences if it is to be accepted. The main one is that there must be a life after physical death, in which there can be further progress towards the full fellowship with God which is promised. Sin must eventually be fully eliminated, and it appears that this does not happen during earthly life.

If salvation is to be possible for all, and if sin is yet to be condemned and punished in some way, then there must also be the possibility of repentance and spiritual growth after physical death for those who have turned away from God during their earthly lives. Some humans may choose not to be among the saved, because they choose things that are opposed to the love of God. If they choose hatred, greed, and egoism, the Bible is fairly clear that they will face judgment of some sort. But if the judgment is that of an endlessly loving God who desires that all humans should be finally united to God, it would seem that the judgment should always aim at the repentance and the reformation of the sinner, and it should not be endless and unredeemable. Such a notion of judgment would, it seems, ensure that sinners would in some way come to face the harm they have done to others, and find themselves in a world of other beings like themselves, a world of hatred, fear, and despair, that their own choices have created. Hating others, and confronted with others as hateful as themselves, they might come to hate themselves, and come to hate life itself. A merciful God would make it possible for them to repent, and learn the ways of love. But it is possible that, if they refuse to reform, they might at some point, by their own choice, choose not to exist.

I could accept such a position as long as it was clear that a loving God would never cease to offer, as long as finite souls exist, the real possibility of repentance and new life, whether in this life or another. It is hard to know what Barth thought. His position remained unclear enough to make his followers unsure of what he really thought.

If there is real freedom, and people refuse to accept the love of God for themselves, then when all evil, suffering, and sin are abolished, in the final coming of the kingdom, such people will presumably cease to be.

None of these consequences are to be found in that form in Bible, which may be one reason Barth did not give a whole-hearted endorsement to universalism. They are, to be honest, philosophical, even metaphysical, theories which are based on imagining what a wholly loving God would do with the millions of humans who have not been Protestants, or Christians, or Hindus, or even morally serious human beings, during their lives. There are clues to this sort of thinking in the Bible,[19] but there is no doubt that Biblical statements about the resurrection of the dead, divine judgment, and the 'end of all things' do not say anything exactly like this.

It is what might be called a conditional universalism, one which makes it possible for all humans, however monstrous, perverse, and evil, eventually to repent and be brought to loving fellowship with God. Barth does not explain how it is that thoroughly evil people could be forgiven by God even if they show no evidence of repentance and faith in their earthly lives. My judgment is that he really wanted it to be true that all would be saved, but could not bring himself to affirm this unequivocally as a truth of faith. This accords with what he wrote in 'The Humanity of God': 'one is to detect no

[19] I try to spell these out in my *What the Bible Really Teaches* (London: SPCK, 2004 and New York: CrossRoad Publishing, 2005), chapter 9.

position for or against that which passes among us under this term [universalism]'.[20]

It is possible that Barth said this because the audience his lecture was given to was a meeting of the Swiss Reformed Ministers' Association, and he would have been aware that many of them would have regarded universalism as a Christian heresy. Or he could have meant that he himself did not have a view about it. Maybe it was enough that Christ had died to save humanity, and only God knew which individual humans would be saved, and under what conditions.

So what is the change in Barth's thought? It could be seen as quite radical – a clear assertion of universal salvation – or rather as one of emphasis – concentrate on the glorious destiny that God offers all humans rather than on the miserable fate that awaits those who are lost in sin. Some scholars, like Tom Greggs, think that universalism is at least implicit in Barth's work, and that it can fairly claim to be an extension of it.[21]

But it is not an extension that Barth himself makes. It is his unclarity on this point that prevents giving a fully coherent account of Barth's thought on these matters.

Creation

The chapters on religion in the *Church Dogmatics* end with a summary outline of 'the true religion', under the four headings of creation, election, justification, and sanctification. It is slightly surprising to find that Barth does not discuss the creation of the universe or of humanity under the heading of creation. If he had, he might not have been so ready to regard humans as damned and contemptible – as he possibly later saw.[22]

---

[20] Ibid., p. 61.

[21] Greggs, *Theology against Religion*, chapter 5.

[22] Barth, *The Humanity of God*, p. 51: 'He does not despise men but in an inconceivable manner esteems them highly just as they are.'

When he speaks of creation, Barth has in mind the fact that Christianity is 'an act of divine creation ... the name Jesus Christ alone created the Christian religion' (144). It might seem odd that a name could create anything. But Barth clarifies this by saying that 'sharing in the life of the Son of God ... is precisely the name Jesus Christ' (145). The Christian religion begins and is sustained by sharing in the life of the eternal Son, by being taken up into the eternal reality through whom the universe was created and in whom the universe will be fulfilled.

As the church is the body of Christ, so the historical Jesus was the human body and mind of Christ. Further, parts of the New Testament state that all creation will be in a way the body of Christ, since it will be united in Christ.[23] That cannot possibly mean being united in a human person. This is a cosmos-including Christ. The human Jesus is the human exemplification of the cosmic Christ. And the church is 'the earthly body of Christ' (146), the Eternal Word, and is not just another religious institution, which may or may not be superior to other forms of human religiosity.

The church is not just a humanly invented society of the like-minded, or a form of religious piety (the worship of a higher reality, or some sort of numinous feeling, as in Rudolf Otto, or sense of the Infinite, as in Schleiermacher, for instance). All such ideas, which Barth sees as espoused by the German liberal theologians, will deprive the Christian churches of life and vitality. Without their real participation in the eternal Word of God they will become something like instances of a 'rather contentedly untroubled religious Hellenism of Jewish, oriental and occidental provenance and colouring' (145). As such, they are destined to be superseded and die.

This is a doctrine of humans sharing in the life of the cosmic Christ, which is very hard to reconcile with Barth's description of humans as 'wholly and completely opposed to God'.[24] It sounds as

[23] Ephesians 1, 10.
[24] Barth, *Church Dogmatics*, volume I, part 2, p. 132.

if only members of a church, those who consciously share in the life of Christ, will be free from divine condemnation. The creation of the Christian religion is a new creation which leaves all other faiths under the condemnation of God.

I have two main comments to make on this passage. The first is that I think Barth is importantly right in saying there is a cosmic Christ, the Eternal Word, whose nature is self-giving love; that Jesus is the human image of this cosmic figure; and that as such, Jesus is the liberator of humanity from sin and the Lord of a coming human community of love. In these respects, despite the fact that this book is very critical of much of Barth's theology of religion, there are insights in Barth which are of great theological value.

But when it comes to thinking about religion, his view of the exclusive truth of one form of Christian religion is strangely restrictive. It is at odds with his own insight that Jesus shows God to be unlimitedly loving. There is no reason why such a God would condemn all religions and confine authentic revelation to a small part of humanity, while regarding all other religions as perverse products of human reason and imagination.

The Barthian positive affirmation entails a number of presuppositions – that there is a transcendent spiritual reality (God); that Jesus' life is correctly interpreted as the life of a non-judgmental saviour; that in and through Jesus God makes a universal covenant with all humanity; and that there is a divine Spirit who makes the risen Jesus known in human hearts and minds. This means that revelation is more complex and more intertwined with human reflection and reasoning than a passive reception of divinely given truth.

It involves a number of propositional beliefs which are all highly disputed. And so they are most plausibly seen, even by those who think them true, as of more or less the same status as many other competing beliefs about religion and revelation. Jesus is one image of a transcendent spiritual reality among others. This, after all, would be precisely the 'liberal' claim that Barth strongly opposes. But it seems to follow from any claim that Christ is concerned with the salvation of all humans, and not with just the relatively small number of adherents of one contested version of Christianity, a version which Barth seems to regard as uniquely God-created. This is an unresolved tension in Barthian theology.

My second comment is that it is quite unfair to see liberal theology as having no moral compass, and as inevitably leading to apostasy and unbelief. Barth's unfortunate experience with the 'German Christians' who swore allegiance to Hitler is a case of the failure of liberalism, not its predictable consequence.

When John Hick – routinely castigated by Barthians – discusses the criteria of authenticity of religious views, he makes the main and over-riding criterion the extent to which a religion supports a morality of universal and self-giving love.[25] That is a safeguard against the evils of religion – repression of other beliefs, violence, anti-rationalism, and hatred of others. There are such evils, but the battle against them is not between 'religion' and 'revelation'. It is between religions of universal love (and sharing in the life of Christ is surely one) and religions of the repression or even destruction of all dissenting beliefs.

Since the Christian God loves all creation, without exception, it is misleading to say that only one sort of Christianity is true and brings salvation. One could say that many (probably not all) of its claims are true. There is no need to make a radical and absolute disjunction between it and other religions. Indeed, it would both be uncharitable and triumphalist to do so. It would also place unacceptable limitations on the scope of divine grace which, Christians could say, is normatively, but not exclusively, expressed in the person of Jesus Christ.

Election

The church is the body of Christ on earth, and in his exposition of the doctrine of election, Barth stresses that people do not choose

---

[25] See John Hick, *The Fifth Dimension* (Oxford: Oneworld, 1999), chapter 18, 'The Criterion'.

the church, but are chosen by God to be the church, not for any reasons of merit or worthiness, but simply by the will and predestination of God. As the sun shines on some places but not others, so God chooses some to be elect without reference to the nature or attributes of those who are chosen. Because Christians are chosen by God, it is not true to say that people choose to become Christians. 'Their decision is nothing but the acknowledgment of a decision already made regarding them' (152). By eternal decree God predestines those who are called, and they can only 'choose their chosenness'.

The idea of election is a challenging but unavoidable one for Barth and for all Calvinists. It is firmly founded on certain Biblical texts, though those texts are qualified by the many other passages that stress the personal responsibility of humans for their actions.

My own leading axiom, like Barth's, is that God is a God of universal and unlimited love. This means, among other things, that God has a purpose for every human life. Some purposes are of extraordinary significance historically, and others are not, though they are still of great importance. Many people feel that they have a vocation, or are 'called', to specific roles or tasks. The Bible records that Abraham was called by his God to leave a great city and travel to a far country.[26] According to the record, Abraham was not an enemy of grace, but a devout worshipper of his God, and he obeyed what he took to be a calling. It seems that the Middle Eastern world, with its many gods, was pregnant with the possibility of developing a monotheistic faith. Although Abraham's faith was probably not fully monotheistic at that stage, his God made a promise that Abraham would be the father of a great people, on condition of his obedience to God's commands.[27]

As theists, we might say that at each stage of each human life and each human culture, in the mind of God there is a preferred future,

[26] Genesis 12, 1.
[27] Genesis 17, 4.

or maybe more than one, which God calls individuals to realise. Individuals are free to accept this preferred possibility, or instead to opt for a more self-regarding future. That is their responsibility. God does not predetermine it, though God may predetermine what futures are preferable, and even predetermine, in a general way, what the end state of the process will be (the triumph of love).

I believe the Old Testament record, taken overall, has close affinity with such an understanding. The descendants of Abraham would over many generations develop a monotheistic idea of a God who had a moral purpose for the world. This would become the idea of a specific tribal nation, the Jews, who had the vocation of loyalty to this one God, and of establishing a nation of justice and peace. As it turned out, world events conspired against this calling, and the Jews often acted in ways opposed to the will (the preferred possibility) of God. The history of Israel is the story of obedience to God interwoven with continual revolt against God's will, and not a story which says that everything that happened was what God unilaterally decreed. Nor was it a story which says that every human action was a revolt against God.

In the New Testament, there is an account of how Jesus, the Messiah, or leader and liberator of Israel, formed a new and potentially universal community of obedience to God, with a vocation to carry the news of God's forgiveness to the whole world.[28] This community, actualised in a variety of institutions or churches, saw itself as the body of the divine Christ, who had been authentically manifested on earth in Jesus. As such, they were an elect, given the vocation and calling by God to make the presence of Christ known in their words and deeds.

Given such an understanding, it would not quite be true to say that people were chosen by God to form the church without regard to their characters and historical possibilities. It would not be true to say that God changelessly decreed their response from eternity.

---

[28] Matthew 28, 18–20.

It would be true to say that people were not chosen for their intelligence or sanctity alone. But those who were 'chosen' were those who were predisposed to faith, who lived at a time and in a place where membership of the church was a real and perhaps a preferred possibility for them, and who freely tried to realise this possibility. They did 'choose their chosenness'. But their chosenness was not fully predetermined; they could have refused it. And it was not without regard to their historical position and the natural possibilities open to them.

I think that only such an account is able to say that God's election without regard to merit was not just arbitrary. It had good reasons, but those reasons were largely concerned with the preferential possibilities of specific historical situations rather than their own excellences. Barth has a real, and I think unsolved, problem of how God's choice can be without regard to merit and yet not arbitrary. He insists that 'the justification of the Christian religion is a just one' (156), and yet refuses to accept any historical or human factors that might have made God's choice non-arbitrary. He relies on the inscrutability of the divine will.

He does say, however, that what is vital is 'the becoming one of the eternal divine Word with human nature' (157). The choice of Jesus to be united to the divine Word was not arbitrary. It required a long process of preparation, so that Jesus would be born into a monotheistic society, one which sincerely worshipped God, and in which the hope of a Messiah was present. It required the realisation of the preferred possibility at a specific time of a sinless life, and the existence of some people who were looking for the coming of the Messiah. God was thus actively involved in the process of development which prepared the way for the coming of the Lord. Providential guidance was involved at every stage, and the strengthening of a community of people who would keep the torch of faith alight even in times of moral corruption. This means that God's election of the Jews might have been without regard to merit, but it was not without regard to historical conditions in which the

Incarnation of the Word became a living possibility in one developing historical community. God's election, or choosing of a developing community of faith, was not arbitrary or without regard to historical conditions. For Christians it was always directed towards the realisation of the Incarnation of the eternal Christ, and beyond that to the realisation of a community which would become the body of the risen Christ in the world, and beyond that again to the final unity of all things in Christ.

The Existence of Evil

God may well have predestined that such things would happen. But a major problem for Barth and any Calvinist is how, if all things are predestined by God, it is possible for humans to rebel against God, and become enemies of grace. If predestination is absolute, so that God is the sovereign Lord, in the sense that God decrees absolutely everything that happens in creation, then how can it be that humans can rebel against God? It seems absurd to say that God decrees that created persons should rebel against God, for then, in rebelling against God, they would be carrying out God's will. And how could God will that persons should rebel against his will?

Barth often places a lot of emphasis on human choice. In his lectures 'Dogmatics in Outline' he writes, 'Faith means choosing between faith and unbelief.'[29] It does not make sense to say that God determines and makes it the case that many people (all people, according to Barth) choose unbelief. A wise, powerful, and loving God could not cause people to choose unbelief, worldliness, and hatred, and be damned for ever. Barth seems to accept this. He says, 'What is not good God did not make', 'We must not look for darkness in God.'[30]

[29] Barth, *Dogmatics in Outline*, p. 29.
[30] Ibid., p. 57.

Yet darkness and unbelief exist. Since they are actual, they are also possible. All possibilities exist, as possible, in God. I imagine that this is a necessary truth. Part of the knowledge of God must be a knowledge of all that is possible. It is plausible to think that if the possibility of beauty exists, then the possibility of ugliness must exist. If pleasure is possible, then so is pain. The whole set of possible states of being is necessarily what it is, and all possibilities, good and bad, exist in God. Maybe God would never realise them. But they have been realised. If God would not realise them, and all things are created by God, then God must have created something that did realise them, some being or beings which can realise possibilities that God would not realise. There might be possibilities that God commands beings not to realise, yet such a command implies the possibility of disobedience.

The mythical story of the tree of knowledge in the Garden of Eden gives an example of such a divine command. Adam and Eve are commanded not to eat the fruit of that tree. But they can do it; that is a possibility for them. The story perhaps expresses the truth that humans can realise possibilities from the divine mind which God commands them not to realise. Yet God has given them the power to disobey this command.

Barth confuses the issue by saying, 'Man's freedom to decide ... is not a freedom to decide between good and evil.'[31] I think he means that a perfectly rational choice, unaffected by selfish passions, would be to choose love and happiness. It is odd for Barth to appeal to reason at this point, when he seeks to reject it as a basis for faith. What he says is that 'the creature makes a different use of his freedom than the only possible one', but that makes no sense. He says that man falls 'by the impossibility of this disobedience, into this possibility not foreseen in creation'. Here the contradiction is clear. Disobedience is impossible, yet it is a possibility not foreseen (even by God?). Disobedience is either possible or impossible; you cannot have it both ways. Since it occurred, it is obviously possible, and since God knows all things, God obviously foresaw that it was possible.

So what does Barth mean? He says, 'evil – death, sin, the Devil and Hell – is not God's creation, but rather what was excluded by God's creation'.[32] Some of the most obvious and troubling things about our world were not created by God.

A clue lies in his statement that 'the creature is threatened by the possibility of nothingness ... which is excluded by God'.[33] This can only mean that there is a possibility of nothingness, but it will never be realised by God. Chaos, the *tohu wa bohu* (the vast deep), is 'the danger by which the world that God created is continually threatened'.[34]

This talk of exclusion and threat entails that there is something threatening and excluding. Calling it 'nothing' or 'impossible' is utterly misleading. There are real possibilities which will frustrate the divine will for creation. Those possibilities must exist in God, but they can only be realised by powers which are able to resist the divine will.

Two main things are entailed by this. First, there are created beings which have the power to realise negative possibilities which exist in the mind of God. And second, God does not exercise a sovereign and all-determining will in creation. Not everything that happens is what God positively ordains. The free realisation of evil possibilities in God cannot be positively willed by God. But God can will the creation of beings which can realise evil. There must be good reason for this. We cannot grasp fully what this is (we are not omniscient). But it almost certainly has something to do with the importance of human autonomy, freedom, the development of excellence in the face of difficulty and effort, and the reconciliation to God of even negative realisations of being which are involved in

[32] Ibid., p. 57.
[33] Ibid., p. 56.
[34] Ibid., p. 48.

some sorts of good. God has a preferred goal for the whole creation, and has preferred possibilities for every situation. But creatures are free to realise futures that frustrate God's providential will.

However, a loving God would always, endlessly, give creatures the possibility of turning back to God in faith. Forgiveness and progress to a more positive life, a shaping of the mind on the pattern of Christ, and the inward presence of the Spirit of Christ itself, would bring them progressively nearer to the knowledge and love of God. In the end, all who do not consciously and knowingly reject love and reject a God of love will be able to share in the communion of souls which it is the predestined goal of the universe to realise.

In this world, communities of faith (the church in its various forms, not just Evangelical Protestantism) would be chosen by God to be reconcilers of an estranged world to God and proclaimers of an eternal and indestructible hope for all humanity. That is the election or vocation of the Christian churches.

Justification

Barth says that those who are 'chosen' to form the body of Christ in the world, continuing Christ's work of reconciliation of humanity to God, are also those whose sins are forgiven. They share in the Spirit, who mediates the risen life of Christ to them. As with election, Barth says that such forgiveness is not based on any human achievements or properties that might justify forgiveness. Forgiveness is given just by the free decision of God.

Barth argues that if Christians 'partake in the human nature of his [God's] eternal Son ... then their sins are forgiven' (158). If this is true, he says, then 'the sin of their religion is also rightly forgiven'. Unfortunately, it is logically invalid to move from the sins of Christian individuals to the sin of a religion. It is false that if the sins of many individuals are forgiven, then the sin of the community of which they are part is forgiven. If religion was simply the sum of all the individuals in it, that may pass. But Barth says that if the Christian religion is 'only a mask', then it is 'falsehood and wrong, an abomination before God' (158). There do seem to be Christians (maybe many of them) for whom their faith is only a mask – thus the long history of the sins of the churches. A religion may be false and faithless, while many, but not all, of its members are forgiven sinners.

He goes on to say that if the sin of a religion is forgiven, then that religion is justified, and is regarded as without sin. This entails that it is the true religion. Again, this a logical non sequitur. There is no logical connection between being without sin and being without error. Even sinless beings may fall into error through no fault of their own (if, for instance, they have been told something errone-ous by someone they have every reason to trust). There is no logical move possible from Christian sinners being forgiven to their reli-gion being the true one.

A more serious problem is that, if the forgiveness of sins is by the free decision of God, without any conditions, then even belief in Jesus as saviour or sincerely believing membership of the Christian church would not be a condition of justification. God could just forgive everyone. Barth even hints at this possibility when he speaks of 'God against and for all men, the whole of humanity' (159). For a moment, there looms the idea that the true Gospel is that God judges and yet is prepared to forgive the whole of humanity.

Yet Barth also seems to say that Christianity is the only true religion, which means that only this religion becomes the body of Christ. It is only by sharing in the body of Christ that sins are forgiven (158). Therefore it is of vital importance to be sure that Christianity is indeed the true religion. Then Barth says that only God could give such assurance. If Christians put their faith in 'ecclesiastical institutions, in theological systems, in inner experi-ences, in moral transformations in the lives of individual believers, or in world-altering effects of Christianity' (159) to justify their con-fidence in the truth of Christianity, that will result in uncertainty, and they will not be able to defend themselves against overpower-ing scepticism. All such factors belong to reason or culture, and so are 'a resumption of faithlessness', and 'the viability, health, and strength' of Christianity will be at an end.

Generalising these points, no one will be able to justify their religion by appeal to any of these factors – the strength of their community, the impressiveness of their theology, the vividness of their personal experiences, the morally transforming effects of their faith, or the social benefits it may bring about. That is because only God can justify, or make true, a faith, and make it unshakeably certain and proof against all the changes and errors of reason and culture.

It seems to me, however, that the only way of knowing that God justifies a faith is to appeal to precisely the factors so helpfully listed by Barth. Since these factors may lead to a positive conclusion in the case of more than one religion, it would be reasonable to say that many religions are more or less in the same boat, and the human search for repentance, trust, hope, and obedience, which is widespread in many (but not all) religions throughout the world, is not an abomination before God. They are genuine approaches to God, which, Christians ought to say, will be met with a grace and forgiveness which are not limited by any requirement of happening to believe exactly the right things or being in the right church. Justification, the forgiveness of sins, is the free gift of God to all, without exception.

It may seem unreasonable, however, to say that even people who have spent all their lives hating God and their fellow humans can just be forgiven. There is a condition for forgiveness, after all, and it is repentance and trust in God. If God is to save all people, there must be some way in which this could happen. It does not seem to happen in the lives of millions of human beings. Barth does not give a clear view of what this way is, and for that reason it remains an aporia, a perplexing difficulty, in his account of justification.

Sanctification

If the Spirit is active in not only forgiving, but also in sanctifying, humans, it should make some observable difference to their lives.

Barth accepts this, since sanctification cannot be an empty word, but entails some sort of actually becoming holier, however fitful and partial that may be. As he says, sanctification is 'sinners brought under discipline' (165). If human salvation is to consist in a fellowship of love and in devotion to God, then those who are made holy by faith must show some degree of growth in love of God and God's creation.

It seems clear at times that for Barth sanctification, as the work of Jesus Christ, is confined to the Christian church. 'It is the sanctification of the community formed by God's revelation, replacing the Old Testament law' (164). As he has said before in these chapters, the Jews were once sanctified by their obedience to the law, but they are not any longer sanctified. Other religions, too, are not sanctified, since all their attempts at love and devotion are still an abomination to God.

If this were true, one might expect Christians to show a moral commitment and a devotion to God that could not be found anywhere else on earth. Anyone who is acquainted with Sikhs, Jews, Muslims, or Hindus knows that is simply not the case. As far as observation goes, there is at least as much love even among atheists as there is among Christians.

It may be true that, since Christians are justified sinners, they might be expected not to go on sinning. But it is very odd that even after many years, most of them do not seem to have improved very much. It seems to be a dogma that flies in the face of all the observed facts that this religious group is more sanctified than any others. This suggests that sanctification is not something that produces sudden and unmistakable holiness. It is extremely rare that it produces the sort of righteousness that was seen in the life of Jesus. John Wesley was one of the few notable Christians who thought human perfection in holiness was possible, and very few have dared to follow him in this.

I do not doubt that sincere Christian faith is able to draw on the power of the Holy Spirit, and that there is such a thing as sensing the presence of Christ enabling one to love God. But I also do not doubt that there is a spiritual power which works similarly in other religions, and is even present, though often unacknowledged, in secular lives. And it is clear to me that the process of sanctification, of greater preparedness to live consciously in the presence of God, is rarely if ever completed on earth.

This means that the empowering grace of God is not confined to Christian faith, even if Christian faith most accurately identifies that power as the Spirit of Christ. And its work is not confined to earthly lives. There must be a continuing growth enabled by grace in the world to come, as the union of human and divine lives becomes closer.

It seems incompatible with the love of God to deprive any human lives of the possibility of forgiveness and sanctification, and to damn hordes of humans to Hell. Barth senses this when he declares that God is 'for all men, the whole of humanity', and that Jesus took on himself the judgment on all humans. If this is true, it is important that people should know about it. So Barth connects with Christian sanctification what he calls 'a ministry of reconciliation' (163), a proclamation of Jesus Christ as Lord to all. The church, which lives by faith in Jesus, must proclaim the hope of eternal life with God to all. This is true but not enough, however. If there really is a hope for all, then even if the church proclaims salvation as widely as possible, there will be millions who have not heard the message, and millions more who, not perhaps fully understanding it, or for reasons which they honestly find compelling, reject it. The implication is, I think, that beyond death the reconciling work of God will continue, and humans will have genuine opportunities to repent, trust, and obey. In the end, all who do not reject God, having understood clearly what God is and promises, will be united in Christ, and will share in the divine nature.[35]

---

[35] I have written three volumes which together set out my views on these issues and form what may be called a systematic theology – *The Christian Idea of God* (Cambridge: Cambridge University Press, 2017), *Christ and the Cosmos* (Cambridge: Cambridge University Press, 2015), and *Sharing in the Divine Nature* (Eugene, OR: Cascade, 2020).

Perhaps what prevented Barth from saying this clearly was the danger that it would lessen the urgency of turning to God, or perhaps he thought it possible, despite his belief in predestination, for humans to reject love for ever. So he continued to say that he did not preach 'universalism'. But he did say, in 'The Humanity of God', 'We have no theological right to set any sort of limits to the loving kindness of God'.[36] The great contradiction that I find in Barth is between his affirmation that God is unlimited in love and kindness and his assertion that all religion and seeking for God, as such, is faithlessness and abominated by God. I find that assertion unwarranted and uncharitable, and devastatingly harmful to the development of a truly loving and compassionate Christian faith. That is why I have written this Critique – and I perhaps need to point out that all the sometimes blunt and even offensive language I have used has been taken from Barth himself, and was used by him to castigate theologians like me.

[36] Barth, *The Humanity of God*, p. 62.

Select Bibliography

Aquinas, Thomas. *The Light of Nature* (Bedford, NH: Sophia Institute Press, 1991).

    Summa Theologiae, Prima Pars, various translators (London: Blackfriars, 1966).

Barth, Karl. *Dogmatics in Outline*, trans. G. T. Thomson (London: SCM Press, 1949).

    The Humanity of God, trans. John Newton Thomas and Thomas Wieser (Louisville: John Knox Press, 1960 [1956]).

    On Religion (para. 17 of the *Church Dogmatics*, volume I, part 2), trans. Garrett Green (London: Bloomsbury, 2013).

Bhagavad Gita, trans. Geoffrey Parrinder (London: Sheldon, 1974).

Confucius. *Analects* (many translations).

Davis, Andrew. *Metaphysics of Exo-life* (Grasmere, ID: Sacrasage, 2023).

Davis, Caroline Franks. *The Evidential Force of Religious Experience* (Oxford: Clarendon Press, 1989).

D'Costa, Gavin and Ross Thompson, eds. *Buddhist–Christian Dual Belonging* (Farnham: Ashgate, 2016).

Evans, David. *Discourses of Gautama Buddha* (London: Janus, 1992).

Greggs, Tom. *Theology against Religion* (London: T. and T. Clark, 2011).

Griffiths, Bede. *The Marriage of East and West* (London: Collins, 1982).

Hardy, Friedhelm, ed. *The Religions of Asia* (London: Routledge, 1988).

Hare, John. *The Moral Gap* (Oxford: Clarendon Press, 1996).

Harnack, Adolf. *What Is Christianity?*, trans. Thomas Bailey Saunders (Minneapolis: Fortress Press, 1984).

Hegel, G. W. F. *Lectures on the Philosophy of Religion*, volume I, trans. E. B. Speirs and J. B. Sanderson (London: Kegan Paul 1895).

Hick, John. *The Fifth Dimension* (Oxford: Oneworld, 1999).

    The Interpretation of Religion (London: Macmillan, 1989).

Kant, Immanuel. *Critique of Pure Reason*, trans. Norman Kemp Smith (London: Macmillan, 1952).

    Prolegomena, trans. John Mahaffy and John Bernard (London: Macmillan, 1889).

    Religion within the Boundaries of Mere Reason, trans. Allen Wood (Cambridge: Cambridge University Press, 2018).

    What Is Enlightenment?, trans. Lewis White Beck, in Immanuel Kant, *On History* (Indianapolis: Bobbs-Merrill, 1963).

Lipner, Julius. *The Face of Truth* (New York: State University of New York Press, 1986).

Panikkar, Raimon. *The Unknown Christ of Hinduism* (Maryknoll: Orbis, 1981).

Pew Research Center. *The Future of World Religions: Population Growth Projections 2020–2050* (Washington, DC: Pew Research Center, 2015).

Phan, Peter. *The Joy of Religious Pluralism* (Maryknoll: Orbis, 2017).

Ramanuja. *The Vedanta Sutras*, trans. George Thibaut, in *Sacred Books of the East*, volume XLVIII, ed. Max Muller (New Delhi: Motilal Banarsidass, 1962).

Russell, Bertrand. *Knowledge by Acquaintance and Knowledge by Description*, Proceedings of the Aristotelian Society, volume XI (Oxford: Oxford University Press, 1910).

Schleiermacher, Friedrich. *The Christian Faith*, trans. H. R. Mackintosh and J. S. Stewart (Edinburgh: T. and T. Clark, 1989).

    On Religion, trans. Richard Crouter (Cambridge: Cambridge University Press, 1988).

Smart, Ninian. *Secular Education and the Logic of Religion* (London: Faber, 1968).

    The World's Religions (Cambridge: Cambridge University Press, 1989).

Smith, Wilfred Cantwell. *The Meaning and End of Religion* (London: SPCK, 1978).

Tao Te Ching, trans. D. C. Lau (London: Penguin, 1953).

Ward, Keith. *The Case for Religion* (London: Oneworld, 2004).

    Christ and the Cosmos (Cambridge: Cambridge University Press, 2015).

    The Christian Idea of God (Cambridge: Cambridge University Press, 2017).

    Christianity (London: Oneworld, 2000).

    Concepts of God (London: Oneworld, 1998).

Pascal's Fire (London: Oneworld, 1996).

Religion and Revelation (Oxford: Oxford University Press, 1994).

Religion in the Modern World (Cambridge: Cambridge University Press, 2019).

Sharing in the Divine Nature (Eugene, OR: Cascade, 2020).

What the Bible Really Teaches (London: SPCK, 2004 and New York: CrossRoad Publishing, 2005).

Wittgenstein, Ludwig. *Philosophical Investigations*, trans. G. E. M. Anscombe (Oxford: Blackwell, 1974).

Index

Index entries generally refer to thematic discussions in the text.

all possibles are in God, 181

Barth and Hegel, 167
Barth on Harnack, 51
Barth on Kant, 46
Barth on Schleiermacher, 48
Barth's paradox, 101, 188
Barth's perverse history of Protestant
 religious thought, 83, 130
Barth's judgment on Judaism, 138
bhakti, 32, 34
Brahman, 30
buddhism and Christianity compared,
 23
Buddhist compassion, 18

Cantwell Smith on religion, 78
church as site of revelation, 9
church as the body of the Eternal Christ,
 174
compatibilism, 107
conditional universalism, 172
Confucianism, 37
criterion of authentic faith, the, 176
critical inquiry in religion, 94
cultural influences on revelation, 63

deciding religious truth, 59
developing ideas of God, 123
did Barth change his mind?, 45
disputes about Christian revelation, 64
diverse ideas of God, 117
diversity of beliefs and salvation, 39
divine and human freedom, 110

East Asian religion, 38
election as divinely preferred possibility, 177
eternal Christ, the, 92

faith as trust, not certainty, 86
forgiveness and repentance, 104
freedom of conscience, 132

goal of cosmic history, the, 183
God and evil, 143
God and moral demands, 104, 151
God as a severe judge, 129
God in Aristotle and Ramanuja, 31
good works as sinful, 103
grace and Buddhism, 159
grace and Hinduism, 163
grace and truth, 155
grace in non-Christian religions, 161, 175
grace offered to all, 139, 187

Harnack's picture of Jesus, 51
Hegel on sublimation, 3
human autonomy and struggle, 182
humanism, 131
humanity as damned and lost, 97
humanity of God, the, 166

image of God in humans, 141
impossibility of natural theology, 82
impossible possibility in Barth, 181
incoherences in Barth, 112

Jesus as stern judge, 92
Jesus as unlimited love, 92

Judaism as incomplete revelation, 69
judgment as reformative, 171
juridical theories of atonement, 127
justification as growth in God, 106

karma, 19
knowledge by acquaintance, 8
knowledge by description, 8

liberal theology, a defence, 54, 133, 150
liberal theology as faithless, 52
longing for God, 119

man as damned and saved, 169
metaphysics and God, 120
modern man, 148
Molinism, 109

Ninian Smart on religion, 56
nirvana, 21
non-Christian revelations, 114, 124
'no-self' in buddhism, 20

panentheism, 30
participative theories of atonement, 127
philosophical presuppositions of faith, 123
polytheism in Hinduism, 34
predestination, 108
Purgatory, 170

Ramanuja, 27, 28
reconciliation with God, 44
religious consciousness, 139

religious studies as descriptive and
    pluralistic, 79
repentance after death, 171
revelation and certainty, 87
revelation and reason, 66, 72, 86, 89, 92
revelation as humanly impossible, 77

Sankara, 27, 28
Schleiermacher, 174
sense of transcendence, a, 50
sublimation as mediating synthesis, 30,
    31
sublimation in many religions, 75

Taoism, 36
'theological' account of religion, 9
theology and religious studies, 81
total depravity, 13, 142
true religion, a grammatical mistake, 58,
    135
Truth and justification, 135
truth and religion, 50, 55, 102

unconditional forgiveness, 184
universal salvation, 130, 165

varieties of revelation, 61
Vedanta, 27

Wesleyan Quadrilateral, the, 90
what Barth means by 'religion', 7
what God adds to morality, 105
world as the body of Brahman, 28

For EU product safety concerns, contact us at Calle de José Abascal, 56–1°, 28003 Madrid, Spain or eugpsr@cambridge.org.

www.ingramcontent.com/pod-product-compliance
Ingram Content Group UK Ltd.
Pitfield, Milton Keynes, MK11 3LW, UK
UKHW020202240325
456635UK00018B/225